National Autism Plan for Children (NAPC)

Plan for the identification, assessment, diagnosis and access to early interventions for pre-school and primary school aged children with autism spectrum disorders (ASD)

Produced by NIASA:
National Initiative for Autism: Screening and Assessment

Ann Le Couteur, Chair, Core Working Group

March 2003

Published by The National Autistic Society for NIASA in collaboration with
The Royal College of Psychiatrists (RCPsych),
The Royal College of Paediatrics and Child Health (RCPCH)
and the All Party Parliamentary Group on Autism (APPGA)

Photographs included in this report have been taken at the NAS EarlyBird Programme
and NAS schools
Designed by Column Communications
Printed by Newnorth Print Ltd

Contents

Foreword

Every parent wants to be reassured that their newborn infant is normal and the discovery that one's child has a serious disabling condition is among the most devastating of all human experiences. Autism is a particularly cruel condition from the parent's perspective. Usually, the child looks physically normal and to the outside world there is no apparent explanation for his/her strange and often disturbing behaviour.

There have been important advances in understanding autism and autism spectrum disorders (ASD) over the past twenty years but autism spectrum disorders still remain baffling and distressing conditions. Recently there has been increasing interest in early detection and early intervention and this, coupled with the growing evidence that autism/ASD are significantly more common than previously thought, created the momentum for establishing an expert working party and the production of this review and report.

The creation of the working party was a joint venture between The National Autistic Society (NAS) and the Royal Colleges of Psychiatrists and of Paediatrics and Child Health, with the backing of the All Party Parliamentary Group on Autism. The latter, together with the NAS, provided financial support for the work. This report is the product jointly of deliberations by both parents and professionals and as such has particular value and significance.

The working party has set out a vision of what a good service for the child with suspected and proven autism/ASD would look like. From the parent's perspective, the intense distress associated with the diagnosis of autism/ASD cannot be taken away, but at least the experience can be assisted by a system that works effectively to answer their questions and provide them with the support they need. The professionals' viewpoint is equally important and their commitment to the provision of this kind of quality service is obvious throughout the report.

It is important to remember that there are many other groups of children and young people with equally serious and distressing disabilities, whose parents also seek a better quality of care and service provision. Examples would include children who are both deaf and blind and those who are suffering from the effects of a devastating head injury. The model of service set out in this report for autistic children is in principle equally applicable to other groups of children with disabilities.

Although there is an emerging evidence-base for the interventions currently recommended for the child with autism, there are still many unanswered questions as to the relative merits of different intervention programmes and the benefits of programmes of greater or lesser intensity. Like so many other disabling conditions of childhood, autism/ASD is a life-long disorder. Yet, as parents know all too well, there has been far less research and investment in studying the optimum approach to care of the adult with autism/ASD.

These are issues that apply to other forms of disability and also to many psychological disorders and to mental illness. Intervention studies have to take a long term perspective but unfortunately research in this field is exceptionally difficult and seriously under-funded. Thus we have to accept, both as parents and as professionals, that we do not yet know for certain how best to provide for all these various groups of children with disabilities, but that is no excuse for inaction – in many places, the standard of service for children with autism/ASD and other disabilities falls far short of the vision set out in this report. Urgent action is needed to provide even the basic standard of care that can be justified by pragmatic considerations, on the grounds of common humanity.

This report will focus attention on the need to raise standards in childhood disability services as a whole, in health, education and social services. It emphasises once again the enormous potential benefits that result from collaborations between parents and professionals. We hope too that it will stimulate interest in the importance of properly funded and expertly designed research, which will enable us to understand more clearly what can and cannot be achieved for children with disabilities.

Dr Sue Bailey
Chair of Child and Adolescent Psychiatry Faculty, Royal College of Psychiatrists

Professor David Hall, FRCPCH
President, Royal College of Paediatrics and Child Health
August 2002

On behalf of our faculty, I am pleased to say that we welcome this document...

In our view, the challenges of autism – one of the most socially excluding of all disorders – can hardly be overstated, especially when one considers its lifelong implications. As a speciality which deals with many adults with autism, we are only too aware of the enormous difficulty many individuals and their families experience in receiving help. For this reason, people affected by autism spectrum disorder merit the attention to assessment, diagnosis and intervention in early life that you recommend.

Professor Gregory O'Brien
Chair, Faculty of Psychiatry of Learning Disability, Royal College of Psychiatrists
July 2002

Core working group

Professor Ann Le Couteur University of Newcastle upon Tyne	Representing the Faculty of Child and Adolescent Psychiatry, Royal College of Psychiatrists (Chair)
Dr Gillian Baird Newcomen Centre Guy's Hospital, London	Representing the Royal College of Paediatrics and Child Health, (Secretary)
Mr Richard Mills National Autistic Society Head Office	Director of Services, National Autistic Society
Dr Rita Jordan (Education) University of Birmingham	Representing The British Psychological Society
Professor Pat Howlin (Clinical) St George's Hospital, London	Jointly representing The British Psychological Society
Professor Sheila Hollins St George's Hospital, London	Adviser to the Department of Health and Learning Disability (previously Dr Oliver Russell) Observer status
Ms Maureen Aarons and *Ms Tessa Gittens* London	Jointly representing the Royal College of Speech and Language Therapists
Dr Tom Berney Prudhoe Hospital Northumberland	Representing the Faculty of Learning Disability Psychiatry, Royal College of Psychiatrists
Mrs Helen Geldard County Durham	Independent parent representative
Mrs Jenny Hugman Neath Hill Health Centre Milton Keynes	Representing The Community Practitioner and Health Visitor Association
Ms Annette English	Representing Educational Psychology and the Special Educational Needs Regional Partnerships
Mr Nigel Fulton	Department for Education and Skills (Observer Status)

Dr Jamie Nicholls
General Practitioner - Essex

Representing General Practitioners

Dr Tony O'Sullivan
Priory Manor Child
Development Centre
Lewisham

Representing BACCH (The British Association
of Community Child Health including the
Child Development and Disability sub-committee of
this group)

Acknowledgements

We would like to thank the membership of the Core Working Group, all contributors to the workshops and all the other professionals, parent representatives, the All Party Parliamentary Group and The National Autistic Society for their contributions to the development of this report. Particular thanks also go to Christine Lenehan from the Council for Disabled Children.

1 Executive summary

These guidelines address identification, assessment, diagnosis and access to early interventions for pre-school and primary school age children with autism spectrum disorders (ASD). It is hoped that they will encourage transparent, efficient diagnostic processes able to meet the needs of these children and families that are not prescriptive but demonstrate good practice.

The guidelines have been published under the banner of The National Autistic Society (NAS) in collaboration with the Royal College of Paediatrics and Child Health and the Royal College of Psychiatrists (see Foreword). The guidelines are for parents and for all who work with children. They were developed by a multi-disciplinary core group of professionals from Health, Education, Social Services, parent representatives and representatives from the voluntary sector.

In the executive summary (and in line with the Royal College of Paediatrics and Child Health summary guidelines for accepted Grades of Evidence) all recommendations are graded as follows:

Evidence
Grade A requires at least one randomised trial
Grade B requires well conducted clinical trials but no randomised clinical trials
Grade C is an expert NIASA Working Group recommendation
An asterisk (*) indicates key points for clinical audit, which should be the responsibility of the local ASD co-ordinating group.

1 **Identification** (See Recommendation 4.1 for justification of all proposed timeframes and details)
Autism spectrum disorder (ASD) affects at least 60 per 10,000 children under 8 years, of whom 10 to 30 have narrowly-defined autism. In a typical local population unit of 55,000 children under sixteen with 4,000 births per year, the number on which resource need has been based in this report, an annual incidence of 24 new cases is implied though presentation may be at varying ages. This in turn suggests that there would be considerably more than 250 children (under 16 years) with ASD at any one time in every such local health area.

Close to 4 per 1,000 children have severe learning disability, i.e. approximately 200 in a typical local area at any one time. Many of these children will have autism or an ASD. Approximately 25 per 1,000 additional children have moderate learning difficulty and many of these will also have ASD. The numbers of children with ASD who do not have a learning difficulty may have been previously underestimated. There is evidence that higher functioning ASD is increasingly recognised (Chakrabarti and Fombonne, 2001).

The benefits of the early identification of ASD are recognised by parents and professionals alike. While there is as yet no suitable test for the universal screening of pre-school children for ASD, the identification of ASD can nevertheless be improved by the increased recognition of alerting signals to identify those children for whom further assessment is needed. There should also be a positive response to parental concerns at all times. Opportunities for identification are available in the home, in early educational settings, in schools and during health care provision.

As ASD is a developmental disorder the presentation will vary with age and, in any one individual, vary over time. The characteristics of ASD may be more prominent at some ages than others. Thus a clear understanding of normal social, behavioural and language development is required among parents, carers and professionals. Existing child developmental surveillance programmes undertaken by primary care teams including health visitors offer a context within which better detection can occur. It is important to remember that ASD may occur in other developmental syndromes including developmental co-ordination disorders and specific developmental disorders and medical conditions such as early epilepsy and tuberous sclerosis. Learning and psychiatric co-morbidities are common.

Identification recommendations

- No whole population screening test for autism (Grade B).
- Training of all involved professionals in 'alerting' signals of possible ASD both at pre-school and school age (Grade C).*
- Regular opportunities (at least at 8-12 months, 2-3 years and 4-5 years) to discuss a child's development with parents as part of 'surveillance' to detect and respond rapidly to any developmental concerns (Grade C).*
- Age of detection/diagnosis of all developmental problems including autism/ASD as a specified disorder to be audited in each local area (Grade C).*

2 **Assessment** (See Recommendation 4.2. for justification of all proposed timeframes and details). Currently, access to assessment is not consistent in local areas or nationally. Parental concern about any developmental problem should trigger referral for a general developmental assessment (GDA) and not be deferred until the next routine surveillance check.

Assessment should be available locally, or at least within the geographical area equivalent to the local 'population unit'. It should be timely and delay should be audited (Grade C).* While many local areas have a child development service (CDS), models vary considerably. Service configuration will be locally appropriate, but for children with a possible ASD, it should offer all the components of the recommended standardised ASD services.

After the identification of concern a three stage assessment framework is recommended, (with Stages 1 and 2 at local level). In some cases stages 1 and 2 may coincide.

Stage 1 - is a general multi-disciplinary developmental assessment (GDA) as for any child with a possible developmental problem. It should comprise the clear identification of concerns, a developmental history, a full examination and appropriate further tests. When considering the possibility of an ASD, no evidence exists to recommend routine use of particular autism specific screening tests although some tests may help identify children who need a further multi-agency assessment (MAA). The outcomes of a GDA should include immediate feedback to the family, even where the diagnosis remains unclear. The family should have adequate opportunity to discuss the outcome of the GDA. Plans for appropriate provision should commence at this stage where possible. The Local Education Authority should be notified at this stage if special educational needs are suspected. Both the components and outcomes of the general developmental assessment should be standardised nationally (Grade C).

Grade A requires at least one randomised trial; Grade B requires well conducted clinical trials but no randomised clinical trials; Grade C is an expert NIASA Working Group recommendation; an asterisk (*) indicates key points for clinical audit, which should be the responsibility of the local ASD co-ordinating group.

Stage 2 - of the assessment process is a multi-agency assessment (MAA). A similar approach will often be applicable to other developmental problems. All the components of a MAA should be applied to all children in whom ASD are suspected since a full picture of the needs of the child and family requires the contribution of all members of the multi-disciplinary, multi-agency assessment team. A named key worker should be appointed at the beginning of the MAA process.

The central feature of the MAA is that it is undertaken by a multi-agency, multi-disciplinary team. The team's core members should be available within a local area, including an educational specialist and an ASD family support worker. The assessment should be completed and feedback given to the family within 17 weeks from referral to the MAA team (Grade C).* Assessment is ongoing. In some children a final diagnosis may not be possible at this stage, but the child's needs should have been identified.

The multi-agency assessment should be capable of assessing the differential diagnosis of possible ASD and providing a baseline assessment of skills and difficulties for both the child and the family.

Essential components for a complete multi-agency assessment (MAA)

1 Existing information from all settings should be gathered.

2 A specific ASD developmental and family history should be taken. No evidence exists on which to recommend any particular framework, but this history should be taken by an experienced team member with recognised ASD training. In some cases it may be useful to use a semi-structured interview such as the *Autism Diagnostic Interview (ADI-R)* or the *Diagnostic Interview for Social and Communication Disorders* (DISCO). If the person taking the developmental history is not medically trained, then the medical history and examination should be completed separately.

3 Focused observations should be taken across more than one setting. This could include tools such as the *Autism Diagnostic Observation Schedule* (ADOS). The focus of the assessment of primary school aged children should include their functioning in an educational setting.

4 A cognitive assessment should be performed in an appropriate setting by either a clinical or an educational psychologist with ASD training.

5 A communication assessment should be made and speech and language competences assessed where needed by a speech and language therapist with ASD training.

6 An assessment should be made of mental health and behaviour. Co-morbid mental health and behaviour problems are common.

7 An assessment of the needs and strengths of all family members should be undertaken.

8 A full physical examination should be performed including appropriate medical tests.

9 Choice of tests will depend on each child's clinical presentation but chromosome karyotype and fragile X DNA analysis are the only current routine recommendations (Grade B). Clinical evidence of co-morbid medical conditions such as epilepsy should be sought but tests such as EEG not undertaken unless clinically appropriate. The evidence base for all investigations should be fully explained to parents.

10 Other assessments may be required to investigate unusual sensory responses, motor planning and co-ordination difficulties and self-care problems.

Grade A requires at least one randomised trial; Grade B requires well conducted clinical trials but no randomised clinical trials; Grade C is an expert NIASA Working Group recommendation; an asterisk (*) indicates key points for clinical audit, which should be the responsibility of the local ASD co-ordinating group.

All professionals involved in an MAA should be experienced and knowledgeable about ASD and it should lead to specific recommendations. A written report should be produced and discussed with the parents and the key worker should be appropriately involved in these discussions. This should include a needs based Family Care Plan (FCP). At this stage genetic implications should be considered.

Stage 3 - is the possible need for referral to a tertiary ASD assessment. The local area team may need this referral for several reasons, including a second opinion, diagnostic doubt, complexity, and specific advice about treatments or key transition stages. Either Stage 2 assessment or tertiary service should include access to paediatric neurology, gastroenterology, metabolic medicine, neuropsychiatry with competences in psychological and pharmacological treatments and other specialist therapy services.

Assessment recommendations (Grade C)

In every local area there should be:
- An agreed written referral pathway for children with suspected ASD, both pre-school and school age, accessible to all professionals and parents: this may be the same as for all developmental problems.*
- A local ASD co-ordinating group for strategic planning of training and service needs/development in each local area with representation from all statutory and voluntary services together with users of the service.*
- A multi-agency assessment in all local areas to be available to families and to include medical, physical, psychometric, educational, communication, language and motor competency, behaviour and mental health assessments of the child.*
- At least one lead clinician in every local area to be trained in ASD and in one of the current diagnostic interviews (ADI-R or DISCO) within three years.*
- One person from each discipline/agency to have expertise in ASD.*
- A clear timescale of response: response to referral within 6 weeks; Stage I (GDA) to plan of action – 13 weeks, and from referral for Stage 2 MAA to completion with Family Care Plan (FCP) after a further 17 weeks.
- A key worker or care manager (as appropriate) allocated for each family with diagnosed ASD.*
- Access to a tertiary assessment available for tertiary opinion work. The tertiary team should be resourced for detailed discussion about specific children, professional consultation and training, and provide a lead in local research, data organisation and analysis.

Interventions (See Recommendation 4.3 for justification of all proposed timeframes and details). The co-ordinated programme of early intervention should be discussed with the family, with support from a key worker, within 6 weeks of the end of the MAA and at regular review appointments. The family should receive information about local parent groups, education and training and information about support services from the family support worker. The child should receive interventions informed by specific ASD expertise. Pre-school children should have access to 15 hours per week of appropriate ASD specific programmes. ASD specific intervention does not necessarily imply segregated ASD provision nor 1:1 working (Grade B). It is recommended that there is a trained professional in ASD in each local area who is capable of setting up comprehensive home and

Grade A requires at least one randomised trial; Grade B requires well conducted clinical trials but no randomised clinical trials; Grade C is an expert NIASA Working Group recommendation; an asterisk (*) indicates key points for clinical audit, which should be the responsibility of the local ASD co-ordinating group.

pre-school based ASD specific intervention programmes. Any other problems identified should be addressed. This may involve liaison with specialist services such as child and adolescent mental health (CAMH) services and learning disability services.

For pre-school and primary school aged children the Family Care Plan (FCP) and Individual Education Plans (IEP) must include clear ASD management strategies for all staff and parents to use, and access to ASD specific individual or small group therapeutic educational opportunities as guided by clinical and developmental needs. It is recommended that every local area should have an ASD trained teacher with resource backing who can visit any school and advise and set up as needed an appropriate IEP.

ASD are developmental disorders and the child's and family's needs will change with age. Professionals need to maintain family contact over time through a suitable team member. More intensive work using a variety of professionals may be needed at different stages in the child's development.

Intervention recommendations *(Grade C unless otherwise specified)*

- A co-ordinated care plan should be produced within 6 weeks of the MAA.*
- A trained professional in ASD in each local area should be available. He or she must be capable of setting up a comprehensive home and pre-school based ASD specific intervention program within 6 weeks of diagnosis.*
- The recommendation is for access to 15 hours per week for each pre-school child (Grade B).*
- Every local area should have an ASD trained teacher with resource backing who can visit any school and advise and set up as needed an appropriate ASD specific IEP for a pupil with ASD within 6 weeks.*
- The key service must be identified for follow up and rapid referral to the full range of appropriate services recognising that needs change over time.*
- A care manager should be identified for longer term co-ordination of the Care Plan for all complex situations.

4 Resources *(Grade C)*

Services for children and young people with ASD require a core investment. For example, for a multi-ethnic inner city local area population, diagnostic assessments by the MAA team for sixty children per year have been costed at £210,000 annually as for June 2002 (see Appendix A(i) p62). Ongoing review, support and intervention, including mental health and learning disability services, have substantial additional resource consequences. These services should be funded using joint budgets to ensure good quality co-ordinated services. In particular the funding of key workers, care manager and professionals for family and home based support and help is needed. Jointly commissioned and funded children's services should be guided by strategic planning.

Strategic planning (Grade C)
A local area ASD co-ordinating group should be established. Its responsibilities should include strategic planning and the facilitation of informed developments; audit and evaluation; local area training for parents, carers and professionals; academic and training links to inform local practice.

Grade A requires at least one randomised trial; Grade B requires well conducted clinical trials but no randomised clinical trials; Grade C is an expert NIASA Working Group recommendation; an asterisk (*) indicates key points for clinical audit, which should be the responsibility of the local ASD co-ordinating group.

Tertiary services should maintain links with referring local area services and agree two-way referral procedures. The tertiary services should be capable of providing specialist multi-disciplinary diagnostic assessments and interventions.

Regional and national priorities should ensure equitable access to transparent ASD care pathways and service provision. New information about evidence based clinical practice should be disseminated and further research should be promoted. National networks are proposed in clinical, research and academic fields.

5

Training *(Grade C)* (See 4.6 for further details)

Joint multi-agency programmes of ASD awareness training on a continuous basis are necessary for all professionals working with children in the community and for parents/carers. All those providing assessment and diagnosis should undergo regular ASD specific training.

Training should be provided for all staff delivering both specific ASD interventions and other interventions for children with ASD. Training should include issues related to understanding ASD and not be limited to single intervention training.

All these three levels of ASD training should be evaluated and audited by the local area ASD co-ordinating group.*

The NIASA working group recommends that a national ASD training committee and network be set up to agree and monitor standards for multi-agency programmes for all these levels of training.

Key actions

1 Easy and transparent access to assessment within a specified time frame.
2 Discussion of the diagnosis, taking into account a sensitive framework for sharing information.
3 Easy access for families to information and support in relating it to their needs.
4 Multi-agency, multi-disciplinary assessment and working.
5 Appropriate intervention.
6 Immediate appointment of a key worker for the family.
7 Care plan developed with and for the family.
8 Care management for complex situations and ongoing needs.
9 Regular ASD specific training of all professionals working in assessment and provision of services.
10 Strategic planning and co-ordination of ASD services for local populations must be undertaken.

Grade A requires at least one randomised trial; Grade B requires well conducted clinical trials but no randomised clinical trials; Grade C is an expert NIASA Working Group recommendation; an asterisk (*) indicates key points for clinical audit, which should be the responsibility of the local ASD co-ordinating group.

2 Introduction and context

2.1 History

Increased public and professional awareness of autism spectrum disorders, concern about rates of diagnosis, and increasing demand for specific investigations and service provision have all clearly demonstrated the need for a UK-wide review. In response to this need a representative multi-disciplinary, multi-agency core group was convened with the support of the Child Development and Disability Group sub-committee of the British Association of Community Child Health (BACCH) of the Royal College of Paediatrics and Child Health (RCPCH), The National Autistic Society (NAS), the All Party Parliamentary Group on Autism (APPGA) and the Royal College of Psychiatrists (Faculty of Child and Adolescent Psychiatry and Faculty of Learning Disability Psychiatry). Its task was to investigate the current UK perspective on ASD provision and services.

A survey undertaken for this report (see Appendix B(ii) p109) confirmed that many local areas across the UK are reviewing current workloads through audit, needs assessments and multi-agency strategic planning. Most initiatives have been conducted within existing resources. The NAS and other interested parties were also concerned about the inequalities of so-called 'post code' driven clinical practice (Howlin and Moore, 1997; McConachie et al, 1999); that families receive very different services depending on their locality and the knowledge and skills of local professionals involved; about length of waiting lists; about the cost of additional demands on existing services rather than an emphasis on cost effective best practice; about clinical governance and other quality initiatives.

The resulting collaborative initiative, the National Initiative for Autism: Screening and Assessment (NIASA), was charged with recommending proposals for a way forward i.e. transparent, efficient, diagnostic processes able to meet local area needs that are not prescriptive but demonstrate good practice.

The Core Working Group was convened in January 2001 and completed the report by summer 2002. The work of the West Midland SEN Regional Partnership (English and Essex, 2001) has also informed the work of this group. The report has been presented to a number of invited audiences, to the APPGA, and the Children's National Service Framework (NSF) Disabled Children External Working Group. The report has the support of the Royal College of Paediatrics and the Faculty of Child and Adolescent Psychiatry, Royal College of Psychiatrists (see Foreword). It has been endorsed by the Faculty of Learning Disability Psychiatry, Royal College of Psychiatrists and all the professional bodies represented on the Core Working Group.

2.2 Terminology

The term autism spectrum disorders (ASD) will be used throughout this report to mean the group of pervasive developmental disorders (PDD) (World Health Organisation, 1993; American Psychiatric Association, 1994) characterised by qualitative abnormalities in reciprocal social interactions and in patterns of communication, and by a restricted, stereotyped, repetitive repertoire of interests and activities. These qualitative abnormalities are a pervasive feature of the individual's functioning in all situations, although they may vary in degree.

It is now generally recognised that there is a spectrum of autism disorders that includes individuals across the range of severity and intellectual ability – from severely impaired to 'high functioning'. This latter term may be misleading in that levels of functioning (for example daily living skills) may not be determined by intellectual functioning. For many 'high functioning' individuals clinical diagnosis may only be made at a much later age.

Autism spectrum disorders are unique in their pattern of deficits and areas of relative strengths. It is not a category within the ICD-10 or DSM-IV classification systems but will be used as a pragmatic 'umbrella term' to reflect the current level of knowledge and degree of certainty of the different syndromes. Autism is defined as the prototypical disorder of the group (see Table 1, p59). Despite the reliance (for diagnostic purposes) on developmental history and direct observation of the qualitative impairments in behaviour, the validity of core autism has been relatively well established and a reliable diagnosis can be made by experienced clinical practitioners at 2 or 3 years of age. However, the broadening of inclusion to ASD has resulted inevitably in diagnostic debate about children who appear to show differing degrees of impairment at differing ages (Bishop and Frazier Norbury, 2002) and those children who have some impairment in the core features of autism but functional impairments due to another disorder such as Attention Deficit Hyperactivity Disorder (ADHD).

Issues of syndrome boundaries remain the topic of some debate and the nosological validity of the sub categories (such as atypical autism, Asperger syndrome, Pervasive Developmental Disorder Unspecified etc.) within ICD-10 and DSM-IV remains uncertain (see Appendix A(iii) p74) for detailed discussion on the conceptualisation of ASD and the importance of considering both diagnosis and the identification of special needs when developing guidelines for this client group). Special needs are of course not static. They can vary with a child's strengths, reflect underlying vulnerabilities and diminish in situations where they are well met. Individuals who meet the current diagnostic criteria for the category ASD/PDD are probably much more common than individuals with a diagnosis of autism (Fombonne, 1999, 2000, 2001). Co-morbid developmental, learning, behavioural and medical problems are common and frequently the most important management issue.

The term ASD provides a clearer representation of the continuity between autism and related disorders within the spectrum (Wing and Gould, 1979; Wing, 1996; Lord et al, 2000) thus acknowledging the importance of the varied manifestation of these core deficits and the need to plan for the assessment, diagnosis and provision of intervention and support services for the much larger number of individuals and their families than might have been previously considered (see Appendix A(iii) p74).

Local population unit

Throughout this report the term local population unit or local area is used. The 'LPU' is defined as the geographical area usually referred to for Health Services provision. The area may or may not be co-terminous with Social Services or Education areas. Such units typically comprise a local population of approximately 55,000 children under sixteen with 4000 births per year. This definition of a local population unit/local area is comparable to the previous health terminology of 'district'.

2.3   Prevalence

Prevalence estimates will depend on the age of the children involved and on the assessment tools and ascertainment methods used. Variations across studies will reflect methodological differences. However, according to recent reviews, there appears fairly good agreement that the ASD affect approximately 60 per 10,000 under 8 years, of whom 10-30 per 10,000 children have narrowly-defined autism (Baird, Charman, and Baron-Cohen, 2000; Scott, Baron-Cohen, and Bolton, 2001;

Bertrand, Mars, and Boyle, 2001; Chakrabarti and Fombonne, 2001). These estimates confirm that ASD is far more common than was previously generally recognised (MRC, 2001). All local area services will need to plan for these increased levels of demand on already over stretched existing services.

2.4   UK initiatives

The work of NIASA has been closely linked with other UK initiatives. A number of the core group members are directly involved in these initiatives.

- National Service Framework for Children
- UK National Screening Committee
- National screening programmes and new developments such as the introduction of Universal Newborn Hearing Screening (UNHS)
- *Health for all children* / David Hall and David Elliman. 4th ed. Oxford: Oxford University Press, 2003
- *Valuing people: a new strategy for learning disability for the 21st century* / Department of Health. London: Stationery Office, 2001
- *Autistic spectrum disorders: needs assessment report* / Glasgow: Public Health Institute of Scotland, 2001
- *Report on autistic spectrum disorders* / A. English and J. Essex. Warwick: West Midlands SEN Regional Partnership
- *Autism spectrum disorders: good practice guidance* / Department for Education and Skills: Autism Working Group. London: Department for Education and Skills, 2002
- *Working party to produce guidelines for ASD* / British Psychological Society (BPS)
- *Together from the start* / Department for Education and Skills: Multi-agency working party for children with special needs from birth to two. London: Department for Education and Skills, 2002
- *Excellence for all children: meeting special educational needs* / Department for Education and Employment. London: Stationery Office, 1997
- Department for Education and Skills. Special Educational Needs Programme of Action (1998-2001) including the *Special Educational Needs and Disability Act 2001* and the *Special Educational Needs: Code of Practice*/Rev. ed. London: Department for Education and Skills, 2001.
- *Standards for child development services:* a guide for commissioners and providers/ Royal College of Paediatrics and Child Health, 1999
- *Disability Discrimination Act 1995*, as amended by *Special Educational Needs* and *Disability Act 2001*
- *Human Rights Act 2000*
- NHS Clinical Governance framework
- Quality Protects programme / Department of Health
- *Framework for the assessment of children in need and their families* / Department of Health. London: Stationery Office, 2000
- NHS Plan modernisation targets / NHS Modernisation Board
- *National Standards for Special Educational Needs Co-ordinators* / Teacher Training Agency. London: Teacher Training Agency, 1998
- Best Value initiative / Office of the Deputy Prime Minister
- *Review of autism research: epidemiology and causes* / Medical Research Council. London: MRC, 2001
- *Right from the start* / Anne Leonard. London: Scope, 1994
- Report of the task group on autism: Northern Ireland, 2002
- *Carers and Disabled Children Act 2000*

- Royal College of Speech and Language Therapists clinical guidelines (in press)
- *Promoting Children's Mental health within early years and school settings* / London: Department for Education and Skills, 2001
- *Fabricated or induced illness by carers* / London: Royal College of Paediatrics and Child Health, 2002.

2.5 Duties and powers of statutory bodies

This guidance reflects the principles contained within the United Nations Convention on the Rights of the Child, ratified by the UK Government in 1991 and the Human Rights Act, 1998. Many agencies have contact with and responsibility for children and young people under a range of legislation:

- **Duties of local authorities**

  The Children Act 1989, section 17, sets out the responsibilities of councils to provide services to children in need and their families to safeguard and promote their welfare. Where there is a disabled child the local council has an obligation to assist the family if they need help in bringing up the child. It is the duty of local councils to work in partnership with families to provide those services that will best meet the needs of the children. Schedule Two, Section Two of the Act also imposes duties on local authorities to set up and maintain a register of disabled children and publish service information.

- ***The Special Educational Needs (SEN) Code of Practice* (2001) and the *Education Act 1996* (the Act)** apply in general to any child. The Act and the SEN Code set out the duties of local education authorities, schools and early education settings. as regards the special educational needs of pre-school children, including children below the age of two, those of compulsory school age and young people aged 16 - 19 who are registered at a school.

- **Duties of Health Authorities and Primary Care Trusts**

- ***The Carers and Disabled Children's Act 2000*** enables parents of disabled children to receive, following assessments, direct payments to purchase care packages.

- **The Government's policy agenda**

  Promoting the well being of children to ensure optimal outcomes requires integration at national, regional and local levels. The Government is committed to ending child poverty, tackling social exclusion and promoting the welfare of all children, so that they can thrive and have the opportunity to fulfil their potential as citizens throughout their lives. A number of initiatives and programmes have been introduced to support families and young children and to raise the profile and importance of early years in child development. Of particular importance for this age group are initiatives such as Sure Start, Children's Fund, Neighbourhood Nurseries and the Early Excellence Centres Programme.

2.6 NIASA terms of reference

The aims of the NIASA working group have been as follows:

2.6.1   To review current UK practice on screening, identification, assessment and interventions for children with ASD using:
- existing evidence based practice
- examples of best clinical practice in the UK

- the advice and experience of the core working group including:
  - findings from other UK and international reports (available up until December 2001)
  - and a literature review.

2.6.2 To take note of the National Service Framework and its aims of:
- improving quality
- reducing variation
- setting a plan of a service model that can be delivered locally, underpinned by clinical governance
- establishing performance indicators by which the process can be measured
- supporting partnerships for service implementation addressing those services that 'allow children to start their lives well and grow into healthy adults, ready and able to play a full part in society' and particularly pertain to the 'cross cutting themes' of 'tackling inequalities and access problems'
- supporting children with disabilities and special needs; involving parents and children in 'choices about care' and 'integration and partnership, including breaking down professional boundaries' (DoH, 2001).

2.6.3 To develop a template that will constitute agreed guidelines for the process of identification, assessment and access to appropriate interventions for pre-school and primary school-aged children with ASD in the UK. This will allow families and professionals to know what is agreed as current (2002) best clinical practice irrespective of location across the UK. The intention is to provide potential models of good practice that will encourage the development of multi agency teams responsible for the identification, assessment and diagnosis (English and Essex, 2001).

2.6.4 To acknowledge the needs of a wide variety of different family groupings from diverse cultural and ethnic backgrounds.

2.6.5 To review and make recommendations for specialist tertiary ASD services and the links that should support locally accessible community local area services.

2.6.6 To propose a realistic framework to meet the training needs for professionals (clinical and research) to implement the recommended guidelines.

2.6.7 To propose timeframes within which professionals should respond to concerns and complete their assessments. NIASA proposes that all local areas should have developed a local co-ordinating group and set up an MAA by summer 2004.

2.6.8 The Core Working Group is aware of the significant resource implications of this plan. It will allow detailed costings to be made for each local area and provide templates for the comparison of local existing services with the agreed guidelines. This document, in conjunction with the NSF for Children's Services, should inform local strategic planning for children and families with ASD.

This work will concentrate on childhood. The Core Working Group recognises that autism spectrum disorders are lifespan developmental disorders and the need for provision that ensures continuity in transition to young adult services. However, this initiative will not consider the needs of adolescents, the transition to adult services nor the acknowledged demand for services for adults.

2.7 Who is this plan for?

- Parent-led groups
- Commissioners/purchasers and providers of children's services: Education; Health; Social Services; independent sector
- Local multi-agency and multi-disciplinary services: Education; Health; Social Services; independent and voluntary sectors
- Legal and advocacy services
- Charities supporting parents and children
- Paediatricians
- Primary care team members
- Psychiatrists
- Psychologists
- Health visitors
- Speech and language therapists
- Occupational therapists and physiotherapists
- Dieticians and nutritionists
- Social Services staff
- Early years workers
- Teachers
- Special educational needs officers
- School and early education setting special educational needs co-ordinators (SENCOs).

3 Key underlying principles for a service for ASD

3.1 General principles

- The implementation of any proposed code of good practice/protocol needs **an environment that accepts and understands ASD**. The proposed protocol requires that the acknowledgement and awareness of autism spectrum disorders is needed for everyone professionally involved with children/young people.

- Early response to concerns should facilitate **early identification** of need and early intervention.

- There should be a **consensus regarding the terminology** used to describe these needs.

- There should be an **ownership of the diagnosis and procedures** by all concerned.

- A commitment to multi-agency working **should be acknowledged by budget holders so that there is a commitment to provide the necessary resources.** This could be facilitated by joint agency funding.

- ASD are complex and it should be recognised that there can be an **overlap of developmental disorders and associated co-morbidity.**

3.2 Working with families

- **Active family involvement** is essential – there needs to be **high-quality, accurate information for the families** which is accessible to families and begins as soon as difficulties are recognised. Provision of information should be seen as a two-way process. It is important that **families are listened to** and that their views and the information they provide are seen as central to the identification/diagnostic process. Support should continue throughout the assessment process.

- The **identification/diagnosis process needs to be transparent** and written information provided where appropriate.

- **Cultural differences should be recognised and acknowledged.** There should be a commitment to meeting the needs of families from all cultural backgrounds, recognising the profound impact that cultural differences may exert for families with a child with an ASD.

- There should be **training for carers (parents and others) following identification** of the child's needs. Access to shared training with professionals in the field should lead to a common understanding of needs and interventions.

- The **views of the child should be incorporated** where appropriate. An advocate should be used where necessary.

3.3   Service provision

- There should be an **identified multi-disciplinary/multi-agency team** of professionals with **specialist skills in ASD** to whom open referral, including by parents, is possible. Teams should be available to assess individuals across the age range. More than one team may operate in the same area depending on the age of the individual being assessed.

- **Communication** between all services is vital. Ideally there should be a **single referral point** to identification and assessment services. All parties should be aware of the key personnel involved and the pathways to referral.

- **Service co-ordination** is essential. Children with complex needs usually require child health, mental health and learning disability services. Professional practice and service delivery eligibility criteria should not exclude children from appropriate interventions and resources.

- **Ongoing specialist support** is vital for the child and family, teachers, carers and residential workers. This will include any further diagnosis and management of co-morbid learning or behaviour problems which may change over time.

- Assessments should always lead to a **Family Care Plan (FCP)/Plan of Action**. Care pathways should be agreed by all and given to parents. The Family Care Plan should be written in a clear format understood by all involved.

- **Social Services should have a central role in the FCP** and planning social support for the child and family. If Social Services know the family then they should be involved from the start of the assessment and diagnostic process. If they are not known to Social Services a referral should be made at any point where the need for extra family support is recognised.

- **Resources should not be contingent on diagnosis** but on an identification of need. NIASA is aware of concerns over 'labelling for resources'.

- **A key person (a key worker) should co-ordinate management** of post diagnostic support, across all agencies including the management of transitions and the sharing of detailed information. The key worker may come from any professional background depending on family preference and the defined needs of the child.

- A **care manager** should be identified for the longer term co-ordination of the FCP for all complex situations.

- Managers should ensure that there are adequate resources to ensure high quality services. The identification process should be continually monitored with **clear guidelines** for **quality standards and evaluation**.

- Local areas should have a minimum of **one nominated individual** from each discipline involved in child health and development, who is appropriately skilled and experienced, **to lead on ASD across each statutory service**.

3.4 Training

- **Specialist professional training** in ASD for staff involved in the identification of ASD should take place both **during qualification and post qualification**. In particular an acknowledgement and understanding of the breadth of the autistic spectrum needs to be achieved.

- **Nominated individuals** should have developed their practice, knowledge and awareness of ASD to such a level that they can **provide appropriate training and consultancy** to colleagues during training and post qualification.

- **All parents and professionals** involved in child health and development **should understand how to access training and consultancy** within their locality.

The text in Chapter 3 is adapted from the work of the West Midlands Identification Working Party (see English, 2002)

4 Recommendations

4.1 Identification

"The identification of autistic spectrum disorders requires expertise, experience and time. If the procedure is rushed and the right questions are not asked, the diagnosis can be missed."

Lorna Wing, 1996

4.1.1 Early identification: whether to screen for ASD

- Although many parents are aware by 18 months that there is a problem, formal diagnosis of autism has been delayed in the past (Howlin and Moore, 1997). Retrospective surveys have indicated that 60% of parents report that they were the first to suspect a problem, compared with 10% who remembered that it was the health visitor and in 7% it was school staff who first acknowledged concern (English and Essex, 2001). Although skilled community staff, such as a knowledgeable health visitor, general practitioner, speech and language therapist, playgroup leader or special educational needs co-ordinator (SENCO), can assist parents to the recognition of a problem, many parents comment that the response of professionals to their expressed concerns, can also be inappropriate reassurance or give the impression that the parents were being 'over anxious'.

- Recent studies (Lord et al, 1995; Lord and MacGill-Evans, 1995; Cox et al, 1999; Stone, Ousley, Hepburn, Hogan, and Brown, 1999) show that a valid clinical diagnosis can be made at aged 2-3 years. However, diagnosis is more difficult in young children who are more able and those with significant general developmental delay (e.g. a mental age below one year).

- Awareness of autism is and has been rising, at least in some part due to recent wide media coverage, and referrals of children aged 2 years are now commonplace, creating a need for knowledge and training in professionals.

- There have been a number of barriers to early diagnosis. These have included failure to recognise symptoms; denial of problem; failure to get referral; waiting time for appointment; inadequately trained staff for diagnosis and; separate waiting lists for each professional group.

- There is a need for a local team of skilled practitioners to whom professionals can contact to discuss symptoms and behaviours of concern rather than providing inappropriate reassurance.

- Most parents and professionals recognise the benefits of early identification and that effective interventions are those that start early and are properly focused for both child and family (Rogers, 1996; Dawson and Osterling, 1997; Lord, 2000).

- There is also an acknowledged need for genetic counselling in ASD.

- Parents express greater satisfaction when they are offered services as soon as possible after concerns have been recognised.

- In the UK, the term 'screening' is defined as the identification of a previously unrecognised disease or defect by the application of tests, examinations or other procedures that can be applied to a whole population. This process results in the identification, with high sensitivity and specificity, of an 'at risk' group. In this report this process will be referred to as **primary screening**. The UK National Screening Committee examines whether certain diseases or tests meet the criteria for primary screening (Wilson and Jungner, 1968; Cochrane and Holland, 1969). In other countries the term 'screening' can also refer to the application of a test or other procedure to an 'at risk' population for the purpose of further refining 'risk'. In this report, the latter process will be referred to as **secondary screening**.

- Screening tests for developmental problems applied by professionals have limited sensitivity and specificity. It is now accepted that parents are able to recognise developmental problems/delay in their children. Parental questionnaires such as PEDS (Parent Evaluation of Developmental Status) can be a valuable adjunct to detection of problems and identification of those who have no problems (Glascoe, MacLean, and Stone, 1991).

- Many children with autism may show qualitative impairments and delays in development from birth but this may not necessarily be recognised by either parents or professionals within the first year. Possibly 1/3 will show a regressive pattern often around 21 months, (varying from 13-23 months) in which word use is lost, and eye contact and social awareness diminish. A very few show normal development to 24 months and beyond and then regress (Volkmar, 1999).

- Screening tests developed for total population use for autism are few. One such test is the CHAT (Checklist for Autism in Toddlers CHAT: Baron-Cohen, Allen and, and Gillberg, 1992). This was administered to 16,000 children by primary care professionals, mainly health visitors, at 18-20 months. Although there was high specificity, (99%) sensitivity was low (38%). Both high and low functioning children with autism failed to be detected by this screening test alone. (Baird et al, 2000).

- Autism/ASD is a group of behaviours with qualitative impairments and delays in achieving certain skills. Screening tests that focus on acquisition of developmental skills will be 'developmental age' dependent. (Scambler, Rogers, and Wehner, 2001) have shown that the CHAT distinguishes autism from developmental delay in referred children aged 29-37 months (mean 33 months) with a non-verbal mental age of 17-29 months (mean 23 months).

- On the basis of current evidence, primary screening for autism and ASD by the use of tests applied to the whole population at specific ages cannot be recommended. However, qualitative abnormalities suggestive of the core behaviours of ASD can be detected in pre-school and school age children. Parents or trained professionals can identify ASD if they have an awareness of normal development and the specific developmental impairments identified in research studies in autism and incorporated into checklists such as CHAT.

- The concept of child health surveillance as practised in primary care/child health services in the UK is a process of continuous dialogue between parents and health professionals (initially in the early pre-school period) that mutually informs about the development of a particular child. The aim is early and prompt identification of any developmental problem. Currently, (*Health for all children*, 4th edition, 2003) no routine tests of development are recommended in the pre-school years.

- Identification of ASD in the population. The NIASA working party strongly recommends that at specific times in each of the pre-school years there is a focus on development by a professional, usually a health visitor, with parents/carers, i.e. during the first year at 8-12 months, then at 2-3 years and 3-5 years in all children, and more frequently if there are concerns. (*Health for all children*, 4th edition, Chapter 18, 2003). In particular, we endorse the use of specified 'alerting signals' (see 4.1.2.8 below).

- Identification of ASD in a child with an existing disability. ASD is an important developmental disorder sometimes associated with other medical conditions such as visual or auditory impairments or early onset of severe epilepsy, yet management of the latter may obscure the ASD. Where one medical/developmental problem exists, especially when the brain is involved, the possibility of another developmental problem or behavioural diagnosis needs to be remembered.

4.1.2 Training implications

4.1.2.1 **Programmes of ASD awareness training** on a continuous basis should extend from health visitors and primary care doctors to all day care/early years staff/the early education practitioner and school/education related services. i.e. to include all potential referrers for GDA. The training should include joint multi-agency and carer training and should be co-ordinated and audited by the Local **ASD Co-ordinating Group** (see Recommendation 4.4). Social communication skills, general development, and the behavioural features of ASD should be recognised as relevant and important aspects of all reviews of a child's developmental progress throughout childhood. Professionals should seek parents' concerns in these areas. The local ASD co-ordinating group should provide a local team of skilled practitioners with whom local professionals should discuss (with parents' consent) concerns about individual children and families prior to referral.

4.1.2.2 Each local area needs to organise and audit, as part of continuous professional development (CPD), programmes to promote increased and continuous awareness of the 'alerting signals' of ASD for community based staff, including all support staff working with children and their families (see Recommendation 4.6: Training).

4.1.2.3 The local ASD coordinating group (see Recommendation 4.4) should review working practice and local area training initiatives with the Regional ASD Network (see Recommendation 4.6: Training) and ensure they are up to date on information about screening tools, assessment instruments and diagnostic developments. This information should be used to inform local clinical practice.

4.1.2.4 Information from studies of the early signs of developmental impairments in autism and ASD can be used in the training of professionals. Instruments developed for screening such as the CHAT are recognised by NIASA as useful training instruments and can help to clarify concerns at the age of 20-24 months (or equivalent mental age).

4.1.2.5 Primary care staff may wish to use a structured form of enquiry with parents (e.g. the PEDS, Glascoe et al, 1991) about a child's development. The use of such schemes needs to be audited.

4.1.2.6 When concerns are expressed by parents about primary school aged children, primary care staff, the school SENCO, or other trained members of the school support staff or the educational psychologist may find tools such as the *Social Communication Questionnaire* (SCQ) (Rutter et al, 2002), the *Childhood Asperger's Syndrome Test* (CAST) (Scott et al, 2002), useful in identifying the need for a more detailed assessment (see Appendix A(ii) p74).

4.1.2.7 Although these and other instruments can be used as **secondary screeners** for the purpose of further refining the 'risk' of ASD in children with **any** developmental problem there is **limited evidence** for the recommendation of their use at primary care level (Baird et al, 2000, Charman and Baird, 2002).

4.1.2.8 Alerting signals of ASD should be widely appreciated and are also useful for training purposes.
- In the first year of life there are usually no clear discriminating features but parental concerns should be elicited.
- Between 2 and 3 years of age concerns in the following areas should prompt referral for a general developmental assessment (GDA) (Modified from Stone, Hoffman, Lewis, and Ousley, 1994).

1 **Communication:** impairment in language development especially comprehension; unusual use of language; poor response to name, deficient non-verbal communication e.g. lack of pointing and difficulty following a point, failure to smile socially to share enjoyment and respond to the smiling of others.

2 **Social impairments:** limitation in, or lack of imitation of, actions (e.g. clapping); or with toys or other objects; lack of showing; lack of interest in other children or odd approaches to other children. Minimal recognition or responsiveness to other people's happiness or distress; limited variety of imaginative play; pretence, especially social imagination (i.e. not joining with others in shared imaginary games), 'in his/her own world', failure to initiate simple play with others or participate in early social games; preference for solitary play activities; odd relationships with adults (too friendly or ignores).

3 **Impairment of interests, activities and other behaviours:** such as over sensitivity to sound/touch; unusual sensory responses (visual, olfactory); motor mannerisms; biting/hitting/aggression to peers; oppositional to adults; over liking for sameness/inability to cope with change especially in unstructured setting; repetitive play with toys (e.g. lining up objects; turning lights switches on and off, regardless of scolding).

4 **'Absolute indicators for referral' (for a general developmental assessment)**
- *No babble, pointing or other gesture by 12 months*
- *No single words by 18 months (Rescorla and Schwartz, 1990)*
- *No 2-word spontaneous (non-echoed) phrases by 24 months*
- *ANY loss of any language or social skills at ANY age*

(Modified from Filipek et al, 1999; 2000)

- **Alerting features in primary school age children**
Professional concerns about more able children, or those with Asperger syndrome/so called 'high functioning' autism, may not develop until children are exposed to the greater social demands of the primary school environment. Indeed, prior to school entry some may have been thought to be well advanced in their development, because of their special interests and precocious vocabulary.

The following features should alert teachers and others to the possibility of ASD and trigger discussion with parents and the possible implementation of the local referral pathway:

1 **Communication impairments:** Abnormalities in language development including muteness, odd or inappropriate intonation patterns, persistent echolalia, reference to self as 'you' or 'she/he' beyond 3 years, unusual vocabulary for child's age/social group.

Limited use of language for communication and/or tendency to talk freely only about specific topics.

2 **Social impairments:** Inability to join in with the play of other children or inappropriate attempts at joint play (may manifest as aggressive or disruptive behaviour).

Lack of awareness of classroom 'norms' (criticising teachers; overt unwillingness to cooperate in classroom activities; inability to appreciate/follow current trends e.g. with regard to other children's dress, style of speech, interests etc.).

Easily overwhelmed by social and other stimulation.

Failure to relate normally to adults (too intense/no relationship).

Showing extreme reactions to invasion of personal space and extreme resistance to being 'hurried'.

3 **Impairment of interests, activities and behaviours:** Lack of flexible, cooperative imaginative play/creativity, although certain imaginary scenarios (e.g. copied from videos or cartoons) may be frequently re-enacted alone.

Difficulty in organising self in relation to unstructured space (e.g. hugging the perimeter of playgrounds, halls).

Inability to cope with change or unstructured situations, even ones that other children enjoy (such as school trips, teachers being away etc.).

4 **Other factors:** Unusual profile of skills/deficits (e.g. social and motor skills very poorly developed, whilst general knowledge, reading or vocabulary skills are well above chronological/mental age). Any other evidence of odd behaviours (including unusual responses to sensory stimuli (visual and olfactory); unusual responses to movement and any significant history of loss of skills).

4.2 Assessment

"The primary aim of clinical assessment is to examine the profile of skills and impairments of the child concerned in order to identify their specific needs. Parents or other carers are partners with the professionals in this process."
Judith Gould, 2003

4.2.1 Accessing the local referral pathway

4.2.1.1 Access

Parents should be able to access information easily about whom they can contact with a concern. The advice to wait for a routine check or 'wait and see' should be resisted. Professionals such as the health visitor, early years worker (e.g. in nurseries, family centres, toddler groups etc.), playgroup leader, school teacher, SENCO, educational psychologist, or doctor who have concerns in the absence of parental worries should have the skills and confidence to negotiate sensitively with the family so that concerns can be discussed and action agreed before referral onwards.

4.2.1.2 **Parental or professional concerns** about a possible ASD, social communication or behavioural problem at any age should lead to the implementation of the local referral pathway usually via a member of the primary health care team. School age children may be referred via the primary care team or the school nurse/doctor, or alternatively by the SENCO or educational psychologist as a negotiated direct referral from the school or an early education setting.

4.2.1.3 **Process and location**
In the first instance, referrals for multi-disciplinary developmental health assessment are usually, but not invariably, to the community paediatrician in the child development service. Depending on the size of the local area and service structure, the referral route may be to a locality base or the area-wide child development service (CDS) or centre.

Each local area throughout the UK has a child development service, though models of service organisation vary greatly. The team should be multi-disciplinary with specific core skills in the assessment of children and families with a possible developmental problem and work regularly together as a co-ordinated group. Some are sited within hospital trusts but most are based in primary care trusts or community health trusts. Child and Adolescent Mental Health Services (CAMHS) also vary greatly in how they are resourced and whether their remit covers learning disability and ASD. Many areas of the country have a child development service (CDS) from which the service is organised serving a child and adolescent population of around 50-60,000 under 16 years (often extended to 19 years).

For children over 5 years without a learning disability referral may be co-ordinated through the local CAMH service in some local areas. For children over 5 years with a learning disability, the initial referral may be made to the Learning Disability service where there is a defined service, or to the child development service, or the CAMH service depending on local arrangements. CAMH and Learning Disabilities Services must be able to co-ordinate a multi-disciplinary developmental diagnostic assessment and provide the health assessment required for diagnosis. At the moment such arrangements lead to a diversity of care pathways for families who receive a different type of service depending on whom they see, rather than on the presenting problem. All parents comment on the need for a clear accessible service which addresses their concerns and leads to an appropriate needs based Family Care Plan.

The local referral pathway for all children should be discussed and agreed by all professionals, written down, reviewed on a regular basis and audited by the local ASD co-ordinating group. A leaflet outlining the **local referral pathway** should be available (Grade C).

4.2.1.4 **What is assessment?**
Assessment is a process undertaken by gathering information about the health, education and care needs of a child and family. This results in an identification of needs (including a diagnosis where appropriate) and a plan for action to meet the identified needs. It is a process that should meet the needs of the child and the family. The assessment has three specific aims. It should:

- identify the health needs of the child, including consideration of differential diagnosis, establishing aetiology, and provision of genetic advice
- promote understanding and agreement about the potential developmental implications of the condition so that effective educational, behavioural, physical, emotional, social and communication strategies can be put in place to promote development

- address the needs of the child in the family context such that the family is given confidence to provide for the health, learning and care needs of their child, whilst understanding that their own needs (including cultural and spiritual needs) are being taken into account.

For some children the presentation may be very clear and an agreed diagnosis of ASD is made early on. The diagnosis should be shared with parents (and the young person) if appropriate, but all the components of MAA must be completed to ensure a comprehensive assessment of need and an appropriate programme of support can be put in place. For other children, an initial assessment of need may not include a final diagnosis of the cause of disability. Diagnosis usually brings with it information about the reasons for the disability, the possible outcomes and prognosis. It is not always appropriate to offer an immediate diagnosis. Sometimes parents vary in their stage of recognition of a problem or the clinical picture might not be clear-cut. Where this occurs, it is important that the uncertainty should be acknowledged and that this should not be a barrier to service provision. Children and families should not have to wait upon definitive diagnosis before obtaining the support they need. The value of assessment should be gauged by the timeliness and appropriateness of the framework for action that is implemented. This framework should be regularly reviewed and audited by the local ASD co-ordinating group.

4.2.1.5
Timeframe for assessment (Grade C)

Throughout this report, the recommended timeframes have been agreed by the Core Working Group after wide consultation with UK colleagues and close reference to the existing literature. The working group acknowledge that there are significant resource implications to the successful implementation of these agreed timeframes.

The **recommendation** is that the first professional contact with the parents following referral to the CDS or CAMHS is **within 6 weeks of the date of referral** and that the time period for the GDA assessment process to action plan (Stage 1) should be completed within **13 weeks**. The **local ASD co-ordinating group** should audit the timeframe and access to the general developmental assessment to avoid delays in families receiving an initial appointment.

Table 2 Timeframe for Assessment (see Appendix A(i), p60)

Figure 1 Pathways for Referral (see Appendix A(i), p73)

4.2.2
Stage 1: general developmental assessment (GDA)

This part of the report describes good practice for any emerging developmental concern regardless of the service involved. The CD services team should take responsibility for ensuring that the initial assessment is appropriate for the child and regularly audit all referrals.

4.2.2.1
Identification of concerns

It is important to document the concerns of the parents as well as the referrer and to be aware of any disparity so that it can be dealt with sensitively.

4.2.2.2
Developmental and family history

This documents the child's developmental history (antenatal and perinatal), and early health and developmental milestones, any relevant family history and information about family functioning.

4.2.2.3   **Paediatric physical and neurodevelopmental examination**
This provides information on the child's current health, including growth, and an assessment for possible dysmorphism, neurocutaneous markers and neurological signs. A baseline profile of general development is completed. Many UK local areas and CD Services use specific instruments for their developmental assessments.

4.2.3   **Outcomes of the GDA** should include the developmental and diagnostic formulation (including differential diagnosis); an assessment of need; a plan of care and a written report for parents; an appointment to review the report; a notification to education made with parental permission if indicated and, if appropriate, entry on the local special needs registry (with parental permission).

4.2.3.1   **Further investigation**
These may include appropriate further examinations including hearing and vision assessment and laboratory investigations.

4.2.3.2   **Outcomes of the GDA if ASD is suspected**
- This should mean referral for a multi-disciplinary/multi-agency assessment (Stage 2: MAA see 4.2.4). In some local areas, components of MAA may have been carried out already during the GDA. All children with ASD should receive all the components of a multi-agency assessment
- Care needs to be taken in introducing the possibility of ASD prior to the diagnostic Stage 2 assessment. However, where one or more professionals experienced in ASD have performed the GDA at Stage 1, and it is clear that the child has an ASD, it may well be appropriate to discuss the diagnosis with parents at this stage.
- All the core components of ASD-specific assessment and management not yet completed, should then be organised. The assessment plan for the child should include the same measures as for a child who has gone through the MAA assessment at Stage 2. The MAA team should be informed about the child.
- Plans to provide appropriate support and provision should commence at this stage and should not await the outcome of the MAA, i.e. the ASD specific diagnostic assessment. **A named professional** who can act as a **key worker** (Mukherjee, Beresford, and Sloper, 1999) (see Appendix A(iv), p91) should, with the agreement of the family, be appointed **within 4 weeks** of the end of Stage 1 – the GDA. This professional should have knowledge of the MAA process. It is expected that for pre-school children this role would usually be taken by for example the child's health visitor and for school aged children the role may be taken by the school nurse or a community based worker. For some children other professionals may be more appropriate. Education funded staff such as an early educator and SENCO may not have sufficient resources and/or opportunities to take on this type of role.

4.2.3.3   **The use of secondary screening tests for ASD (i.e. a test used for a population already at risk for developmental disorders)**
When a child has been seen for a GDA by the child development team, there may be a concern that an ASD assessment is needed. Currently there is no evidence on which to base recommendations for the use of any particular autism specific screeners in the UK. Some ASD screening tools such as the *Social Communication Questionnaire* (SCQ) (Berument, Rutter, Lord, Pickles, and Bailey, 1999; Rutter et al, 2002), the *Pervasive Developmental Disorders Screening Test* (PDDST) (Siegel, 1998) and *Childhood Asperger's Syndrome Test* (CAST) (Scott, 2002) may assist in the identification of those who need an ASD assessment.

4.2.4 Stage 2: multi-agency assessment (MAA)

4.2.4.1 Who contributes to a multi-agency assessment team?

The term MAA has been used throughout this document to emphasise not only that that the team is multi-disciplinary, working in every local area but that the professionals involved must be able to work across existing professional and service boundaries to provide a multi-agency service (English and Essex, 2001). By working together the multi-agency team co-ordinates and determines what forms of assessment are needed, what the goals of the assessment are to be, and clarifies what role different professionals will play. All the essential components of assessment should be provided by local services within local area.

All members of the team should have specific ASD training with at least one member trained in assessment and diagnosis of ASD using standardised assessment tools such as the *Autism Diagnostic Interview – Revised* (ADI-R) (Lord, Rutter, and Le Couteur, 1994; Le Couteur et al, in press) or the *Diagnostic Interview for Social and Communication Disorders* (DISCO) (Leekam et al, 2002).

It is the expert skills and clinical judgment of the individuals involved that are important not necessarily their professional background (West Midlands Identification Working Party – see English, 2002).

Key roles and personnel should include:
- psychological (educational and/or clinical psychologist)
- educational (specialist teacher, or early years professional and/or educational psychologist)
- linguistic/communication (speech and language therapist)
- developmental/medical and psychiatric (community paediatrician, child and adolescent psychiatrist); some teams have a child and adolescent psychiatrist and/or a consultant child and adolescent learning disability consultant in the core team
- other assessments such as occupational therapy, physiotherapy, access to dietician and nutritionist advice, should be part of the assessment procedure; all child development services (CDS) should include occupational therapy, physiotherapy and access to dietetic services
- ASD family support worker
- Social Services should be involved in the care planning and implementation of appropriate early support (Hart, Geldard, and Geldard, 2000)
- administrator.

4.2.4.2 Timeframe
The recommendation is that the period for the Stage 2 multi-agency ASD assessment (MAA) to the feedback to the family should be no more than 17 weeks. As the MAA team plan the assessment appointments, one member of the team should be nominated to collate the information from all the components and be responsible for the production of the written report. This team member should be present at the feedback meetings with the parents (4.2.5) Local services should audit access to Stage 2 MAA and timeframe to minimise the risk of delay for concerned families.

Table 2 – Timeframe for assessment (see Appendix A(i) p60)

4.2.4.3 Components of multi-agency assessment (MAA)
The assessment should provide a differential diagnosis of possible ASD, exclude other recognised disorders of aetiological significance, establish a baseline assessment of skills and difficulties for both the child and the family; identify any co-morbid conditions and produce information which will lead to the production of an FCP.

1 **Co-ordination of existing information from all settings** (with parental consent) to avoid repetition for the child and family. Where this is available before the diagnostic interview it should be collated and made available at the time of the appointment. For example, children with Statements of Special Educational Needs will have already been assessed for this purpose. The LEA will have requested advice from parents, school or early education setting, speech and language therapy, medical, psychological, social services, and any relevant sources. Similarly, for children with special educational needs (SEN) but without a Statement, schools and early education settings should have information about the child's needs that will inform the MAA.

2 **ASD specific developmental history** (see Appendix A(iii) p76) There is no evidence base for any particular framework for history taking. However, a systematic approach to history taking is essential for all children and should include a family genetic history, a lifetime account and a description of the current functioning of the child. Aspects of daily living including motor planning/execution difficulties; sleep patterns; nutritional/feeding difficulties; diet, bowel and bladder function; sensory sensitivities; behaviour and psychiatric mental state should be included. The headings within the ICD-10 diagnostic guidelines (WHO 1993) provide a framework for the ASD specific developmental history. The history should be undertaken by an experienced member of the multi-disciplinary team with recognised ASD training (Recommendation 4.6: Training). Semi-structured interviews such as the ADI-R or DISCO can be used when more information is required for a diagnosis. Training in one of those instruments is valuable (Recommendation 4.6 Training). Where the interviewer is not medically qualified, then the specific medical history and examination must be conducted by a medical practitioner at another time.

3 **Observational assessments** (see Appendix A(iii) p76)

• **Focused observations taken across more than one setting** This could include school, nursery, home setting using an agreed framework for both informal and specific observational recording are recommended. These observations need to be conducted in a manner that is sensitive to parents' concerns. Children with possible ASD may perform very differently in different settings. Observations of the child in familiar surroundings will complement the information obtained at the initial appointment at the child development service and assist in the understanding of the child's profile of relative strengths and weaknesses.

There is no generally agreed evidence-based checklist/framework. An analysis of the child's environment is important when considering influences and factors that might be contributing to the child's behaviour. These observations can provide diagnostic information and help to inform assessment of needs. This information should be obtained from both community and education based staff working with the child and family. For the older school children focused observations will need to be obtained from a broader range of settings, for example, assessment through teaching. Information may need to be obtained from school and education support staff; specialist community nurses other community mental health workers, social work and respite care staff.

Further assessment, focusing on the child's behaviour, daily living skills and level of independence may be aided by checklist or structured interview schedules (such as Vineland Adaptive Behaviour Scale (VABS), Sparrow, Balla, and Cicchetti, 1984).

- Direct observational assessments. A systematic approach to direct observation is recommended to examine communication, social interaction and play skills. Standardised semi-structured assessment tools such as the Autism Diagnostic Observation Schedule (Lord et al, 2000) are available, although training is required and currently limited in availability.

4 Cognitive assessment (pre-school and primary school aged children)

It is essential to establish a baseline assessment of a child's profile of skills and impairments. Although it is sometimes suggested that formal cognitive assessments for this group of children are inappropriate, long-term research studies indicate that if suitable tests are used the findings are both valid and highly reliable, often over many years (Howlin, 2000). Whilst non-standardised observations in naturalistic settings are an important part of the assessment process, these alone may not necessarily reveal the full picture of a child's particular profile of skills and weaknesses. However, generally a single test will not be sufficient (Lord and Bailey, 2002; Leekam et al, 2002). For some pre-school children the parental interview (e.g. VABS) may be sufficient and individual assessment delayed until the child can be more settled.

Although the overall score may be helpful in clarifying the extent of a child's intellectual impairment, it is often the uneven pattern of functioning shown by the child in different areas that is more important in determining educational needs. Children's responses during psychometric testing can also provide valuable information on their general learning style; approach to novel and/or challenging stimuli; behaviour and co-operation in one to one structured settings; memory and attentional skills; motivation and determination; and abnormal behaviours such as perseveration, repetition and resistance to change.

There are many different tests designed for use with pre-school and school age children. However, there is no evidence base on which to determine the most valid tests for children with ASD of different ages, or cognitive and linguistic levels. All tests have advantages and disadvantages and to some extent choice will depend on the tester's particular preference, and the nature of the child's difficulties. Tests with a high verbal loading, for example, are of little use for non-verbal children. Similarly, more information may sometimes be obtained from a less well standardised test (such as the Merrill Palmer) in which the contents seem to appeal to children with autism, than from a better standardised test, such as the Wechsler Pre-school and Primary Scale of Intelligence – Revised (WPPSI), with less 'engaging' tasks (see Appendix A(iii) p79).

Care is also needed in deciding on the best setting in order to achieve a successful cognitive assessment. If it is necessary to adopt non-standardised testing strategies (e.g. while following the child around the room or adaptations to the presentation of the test items), such modifications to recommended procedures should be noted. Assessment should be undertaken by either a clinical or educational psychologist with expertise in ASD. Assessments that rely on parent report, such as the Vineland Adaptive Behaviour Scale or Griffiths Scale, may sometimes overestimate observed skills but do at least make it possible to obtain a cognitive profile for almost all children.

For some children cognitive assessments may be available from the school based assessments. Any additional investigations should complement existing reports.

5 Communication, speech and language assessment (pre-school and primary school aged children)

An initial framework of assessment (Aarons and Gittens, 1992) should include communication strategies, social interaction and joint attention; learning potential and preferred learning style;

readiness to engage, listen and attend, and play skills, as well as receptive and expressive competencies. It should be undertaken by a speech and language therapist with ASD training or another professional with explicit training in this field.

The choice of language assessments used will depend on individual factors within the child (see Appendix A(iii) p81). These assessments do not provide a comprehensive picture of the child's overall communication skills and the information they provide must be viewed qualitatively together with more informal but semi-structured techniques in order to evaluate a child's social understanding and pragmatic use of language.

Primary school aged children The focus of assessment will need to include their functioning in an educational setting. Structured observation periods in both the classroom and the playground are needed to evaluate sitting, looking, listening and turn taking; interest in and focus on classroom activities; general classroom behaviour; participation in class; awareness of others; voice quality and speech difficulty; response to teacher's instructions; spontaneous social communication; behaviour and social interaction in playground.

6   Behaviour and mental health assessment. It is important to include a specific assessment of the child to identify psychiatric and neuro-developmental co-morbidity. In particular, the assessment should consider temperamental characteristics, behavioural and psychiatric symptoms such as anxiety, over activity, impulsivity, conduct/oppositional behavioural difficulties, obsessive compulsive symptoms, vocal and motor tics, mood disturbance etc. There is no evidence base for using currently available mental health diagnostic tools with children with possible ASD (see Appendix A(iii) p82). The CAMH and LD services must have the skills to identify and differentiate ASD, co-morbid developmental disorders and psychiatric disorders. These assessments will usually involve a psychiatrist as part of the assessment team.

7   **Family assessment**
An assessment of the needs and strengths of all family members - (parents /carers, siblings and the extended family) and psychosocial factors should be undertaken by the key worker in conjunction with the MAA team. A Social Services assessment using the Framework for the Assessment of Children in Need and their families (2000) is necessary to agree any further appropriate interventions and support. This assessment will draw on much of the information gathered throughout the MAA (See Appendix A(iii) p82).

8   **Physical examination – recommended assessments in all**
•   Height, weight and head circumference should be measured and charted in all children. Parental head circumference should be measured if child has a large or small head (Woodhouse et al, 1996; Fombonne et al, 1999, Filipek et al, 2000). Hearing and vision should be assessed in all. Questions about diet, eating, bowel and bladder function and sleeping should also be part of the routine history taking. Specific enquiry about any possible fits is needed.

•   Physical examination including a full neurological examination should include skin examination with and without a Woods Light, particularly in response to clinical indicators such as unusual motor movements; any suggestion of regression, fits, skin lesions and significant learning difficulties (Bailey, 2002).

9 Medical investigations

The NIASA working party concluded on the basis of research evidence that medical causes are found only in a small percentage of children with autism (Shevell et al, 2001; MRC, 2001).

Approximately 10-15% of cases of autism are associated with identifiable medical disorders (Rutter et al, 1994; Barton and Volkmar, 1998). However, the association is more often with a somewhat atypical clinical picture as in individuals with more severe learning difficulties (Fombonne et al, 1999). Where a neurobiological disorder is postulated, but no cause is yet identified, parents are naturally impatient to investigate. They may be vulnerable to theories and treatments that have little scientific evidence. Investigations should take place in an accredited laboratory and the resulting treatments should be evidence based. The working group was concerned that families use a variety of laboratories for investigations that frequently lack an evidence base. The evidence base for all investigations (i.e. those done routinely and those not recommended for routine use) should be explained fully to parents.

Further assessments recommended for some children

- High resolution chromosome karyotyping and specific molecular genetic testing for the Fragile X chromosomal anomaly is recommended where there is evidence of significant language or learning difficulty in addition to ASD. If these tests are done in children with normal IQ, an audit of the results should be undertaken. The yield of abnormal results in high functioning children is likely to be low.
- Consideration should be given to testing for Rett Syndrome in both males and females with a history of regression and significant learning difficulties. There is expanding literature about the prevalence and variability of the wider Rett phenotype but at this moment there is no recommendation for routine testing in ASD for MECP2 gene (Kerr, 2002).
- Lead screening is recommended on clinical suspicion of pica and changes of behaviour, but not routinely in ASD.
- Full blood count and film particularly looking for iron deficiency anaemia should be done in any situation of dietary concern (Chakrabarti and Fombonne, 2001).
- Metabolic investigations. None should be undertaken routinely. It is important to consider the clinical history and presentation to determine which investigations would be appropriate. For example the presence of learning difficulties, fits or an unusual clinical presentation such as recurrent vomiting and presentation with variable levels of consciousness should influence clinical practice and might suggest an underlying metabolic disorder.
- Creatinine phosphokinase (CPK) should be estimated in boys with learning difficulties, language delay, or delayed walking (i.e. beyond 18 months) in a child who has crawled (except in clear cases of familial bottom shuffling) and in certain situations of motor impairment (e.g. cannot run/get up from the floor easily).
- An EEG is not recommended routinely for all children, but as part of the clinical investigations when considering the differential diagnosis and a possible diagnosis of epilepsy. The NIASA Working Group recommends a high level of clinical sensitivity particularly where there are accounts of a possible regression (loss of use of words, social withdrawal) in the second year, a fluctuating clinical course where skills seem to come and go or other unusual behaviour pattern or a movement disorder of variable and fluctuating presence. Although epileptiform EEGs are common in autism, with and without regression, there is insufficient evidence upon which to base any specific treatment of an epileptiform EEG in the absence of a diagnosis of epilepsy (for which

the usual antiepileptic medication would be prescribed). A history suggestive of regression, in a previously normal child after the age of 2 years, requires a detailed assessment and a series of neurological investigations including EEGs (Levine et al, 1999; Tuchman and Rapin, 1997).

• Neuroimaging such as magnetic resonance imaging (MRI) and computerised tomography (CT) is not recommended unless there are specific neurological signs or other indications such as consideration of a diagnosis of tuberous sclerosis or in some circumstances, a focus on EEG (Filipek, 1999; Chugani, 2000; Santosh, 2000).

• Thyroid function tests should only be undertaken in children with evidence of significant learning difficulties who were not tested in the neonatal period.

• Although routine investigation of the gastro-intestinal tract is not recommended, an adequate clinical history of bowel function based on standard best paediatric clinical practice with knowledge of normality and abnormality at appropriate ages is recommended. More detailed investigations are recommended in situations of failure to thrive and other clinical indicators of inflammatory bowel disorder (for example, evidence of blood in the stools, ulceration of oral mucous membrane, fever and chronic ill health). Constipation with overflow may need to be specifically enquired for and if present investigated by abdominal examination and/or plain abdominal X-ray.

Not recommended

• At the present time there is no evidence to recommend the routine testing of bowel permeability, blood or urine opioids or peptides, vitamin or trace elements, gut antibodies, sulphate or other metabolic functions. However, these recommendations should be regularly reviewed in the light of new research findings.

All these assessments need to be co-ordinated as part of the MAA and completed within a 4-8 week period. Clinical practice should be regularly audited in all local areas. The local ASD co-ordinating group should review local practice with the Regional ASD Network (Recommendation 4.5 Tertiary Services).

As always in clinical practice if there is an alteration in a child's behaviour a clinical examination as well as a detailed careful history can be helpful. However, it is important to remember that other relevant external events may have occurred. Young people with ASD are as prone to ordinary accidents and illnesses as others and should not be excluded from the general medical preventive health services including immunisation (Tuffrey and Finlay, 2001) and prompt medical investigations that are available to the rest of the population.

10 Other assessments

Occupational therapy and/or physiotherapy assessment should be available to identify and assess functional difficulties of children with sensory needs and problems, motor planning difficulties and motor co-ordination disorders and self-care problems (see Appendix A(iii) p87) for details of occupational therapy assessments).

4.2.5   ## Outcome of the ASD assessment process

Assessment is an on-going process and it is important to recognise that a clear diagnosis may not necessarily be made at the end of the initial assessment process. This should NOT prevent the development of a needs based intervention plan and provision of appropriate support and interventions (see Recommendation 4.3 Interventions). However, as soon as a diagnostic formulation has been made this should be shared with the parents by members of the local MAA team.

Multiaxial frameworks, such as ICD-10 and DSM-IV, provide a means to identify a particular pattern of skills and deficits and consider other relevant child, family and psychosocial factors in each decision (Taylor and Rutter, 2002). The discussion should involve more than one member of the diagnostic team. In many MAA teams this would currently involve a medically qualified practitioner (paediatrician or child psychiatrist) and another professional such as a psychologist, or speech and language therapist. The key worker should be appropriately involved in all these discussions. Parents/carers should be offered:

- An informed discussion about the needs of their child and family which takes into account the impact of a diagnosis of ASD for their particular child and their individual family circumstances. This should inform the development of the agreed FCP for the family.

- Genetic predisposition counselling. This should be discussed with every family. In idiopathic 'autism' it is known that there is an increased family risk of autism (in siblings the risk is approximately 5 per 100) and an increased risk for a broader autism phenotype (20 per 100 depending on the diagnostic boundary). This represents a specifically increased risk compared with the general population risk (Simonoff, 2000). If there is a known medical cause for the autism for example tuberous sclerosis, or Fragile X chromosomal anomaly, the genetic risks are those of the underlying medical condition.

- A written report of the outcome of the assessment, summary of the discussion and the diagnosis and FCP. Parents should be encouraged to contribute to the report and in particular to identify any errors of factual content. The report should be written in a way that is accessible to families and considers the linguistic and cultural needs of individual families.

4.2.5.1   **Timeframe:** The revised report (dated and signed) should be provided within **17 weeks of the start of the stage 2 MAA**. With the parents' agreement, the revised report should be given to the referrer, the key worker, the General Practitioner and health visitor, early education or school staff and the LEA, and/or other local professionals working with the child and family.

4.2.5.2   **Information**

As well as receiving a copy of the report, parents should be provided with copies of information leaflets about ASD, The National Autistic Society (NAS) and Local Autistic Society (LAS), parent and other independent support network and charities such as Contact a Family and locally produced booklets/leaflets that provide written information about **local** multi-agency services.

- The literature about local interagency networks should include information about available benefits (e.g. Disability Living Allowance), education and therapeutic interventions and other resources for families. This information should be available in English and other languages as appropriate. It may be developed as a **local booklet** and updated regularly by the **Local ASD co-ordinating group**. This should be co-ordinated through the information role of the Local Authority, usually now developed in partnership with the *Children Act* register.

- Information should also be given about Local Education Authority provision and SEN procedures. Every LEA has a Parent Partnership service, which provides neutral and factual information on all aspects of the SEN framework and local provision. Details of the service in each LEA are set out in the DfES publication *Special Educational Needs (SEN): a Guide for Parents and Carers* (available from DfES Publications 0845 6022260 ref: 800/2001).

- Information about internet sites, publications, training opportunities, conferences and academic/ research initiatives co-ordinated through Regional networks with local/regional/national/international perspectives should also be available to parents/carers and key workers.

- Information about any further referrals and diagnostic assessments for example to the **Tertiary Service** (see Recommendation 4.5) should be given to parents and key worker if there are diagnostic uncertainties or other complexities influencing the diagnostic process and formulation.

4.2.5.3 **Next steps**

Parents should be involved in all discussions concerning further investigations and/or treatments of any identified medical condition and plans for follow-up of the relevant difficulties.

- Explicit plans should be made for the '**next steps**' in the development of a Family Care Plan (FCP) (Bailey et al, 1990). The co-ordination of interventions and supports for the child and the family (this applies for both those children WITH and WITHOUT an agreed diagnosis) should be outlined, with time scales and dates agreed. The key worker should be available to support the family during this process. For more complex situations, and family with multiplex ongoing needs it may be more appropriate to appoint a care manager. The professional should have ASD expertise and be able to plan and co-ordinate interventions with the family. Particular consideration may need to be given to the future needs of siblings. This may be addressed through the core assessment carried out by Social Services.

- The date for the next review appointment with named representatives of the MAA team should be confirmed, (including a named senior clinician from the 'base service'). For most children the 'base service' will be the child development service (CDS) or equivalent. For some older children the community child and adolescent mental health service (CAMHS) or the learning disability services (LDS) community child learning disability service (CLDS OR CDS) may be designated as the 'base service' to provide continuity of clinical information and care. The care manager may be based at the base service. These arrangements should be reviewed/audited by the **local ASD co-ordinating group.**

- At **subsequent review appointments** the detailed management plan/FCP containing the recommendations for future provision and support should be reviewed.

- Once the initial diagnosis and FCP have been established, there should be a **regular review of the Family Care Plan on at least an annual basis**. Where a child has a statement of special educational needs it is good practice to co-ordinate the review of the FCP with the annual review of the statement. This has significant resource and personnel implications for all local areas/local health communities. Combined reviews will inevitably require more time allocated to ensure that the full range of needs are considered. Representatives from education, health, therapy and all intervention services should be available to attend these reviews.

Continuity of care and access to support throughout childhood is recommended for all children with complex developmental disorders such as ASD, and their families. It is important to remember that there may be more than one family member affected with ASD, the broader phenotype or a co-morbid disorder. This will affect the level of burden of care. The key worker should provide ongoing support to the family and liaise with the named senior clinician at the base clinical service. The child and family may not necessarily meet regularly with this named clinician if the routine management of the child is successfully progressing as identified in the FCP.

- **Parental permission**

Parental permission should be requested to include the child on the Local Health and Local Authority Special Needs register and ASD specific registry if appropriate.

4.2.5.4   **Problems associated with ASD**

It is the responsibility of the senior clinician and the base clinical service to oversee the treatment needs of the child over time and /or make appropriate referrals as necessary to any relevant specialist service. Particular attention needs to be made to evidence of general or specific learning disability; any change in clinical state; onset of additional co-morbidity such as epilepsy, bowel dysfunction; psychiatric disorder (such as Attention Deficit Hyperactivity Disorder; social phobia, affective disorder, Obsessive Compulsive Disorder, Tourette's – this is not an exhaustive list); any evidence of regression; newly emerging behavioural or other disorders, including sleep disturbance, and make the necessary adjustments to the FCP.

- Families should be introduced to other services (including health) as appropriate e.g. **Child and Adolescent Mental Health Services** and/ or **Community Learning Disability Team** or equivalent.

- Resources need to be identified and monitored for each local area. This should be a task for the **local ASD co-ordinating group** in conjunction with the Primary Care Trust.

Table 3: Example of resource costings for assessment: Multi-ethnic population in Inner City location: (see Appendix A(i) p62).

4.3   Interventions

Autistic spectrum disorders should not be regarded as a label but as a signpost to point us in the right direction.   Exley, cited by Jordan 1999

ASD covers a broad group of disorders that share the core deficits (see Appendix A(i) p59) but with a wider range of degrees of handicap and impairment and even, for some, special skills and abilities.

Research has supported the effectiveness of a range of intervention approaches, but there is no evidence that one approach is more effective than others (Dawson and Osterling, 1997; Rogers, 1996; Jordan, Jones and Murray, 1998). The emphasis has been on the effectiveness of behavioural and educational intervention approaches. Further there is some emerging evidence that targeted interventions should begin as early as possible (Harris and Handleman, 1988; Howlin, 2001). Early identification and intervention increases the likelihood of individuals attaining their full potential. These guidelines describe a minimum for both general and specific support and interventions that should be made available. Local areas need to be clear about what they can offer. There needs to be interagency co-operation and the details of service provision need to be made available to families. The range of provision should be regularly reviewed and access to provision regularly audited by the local ASD co-ordinating group.

(For detailed overview of interventions – See Appendix A(iv) p87).

4.3.1   **General interventions which may be common to all disabilities**

Once the child's needs have been identified the child and family have a right to a coordinated programme of intervention to support the development of the child and family. All involved services should contribute to the co-ordinated Family Care Plan (FCP). These services include the statutory funded authorities and the voluntary sector.

The **key worker** (see Appendix A(iv) p91, C p121) will act as an advocate for the child and family with other services, provide support for the family, access information, co-ordinate clinical reviews and transitional planning, attend meetings and review appointments (if appropriate for the family). The key worker model is not specific to ASD and is a model effective for supporting families and coordinating care for complex needs (Mukherjee, Beresford and Sloper, 1999). However, in some circumstances it may be more appropriate to appoint a **care manager** (see Appendix C p120).

Services that are likely to be involved in the co-ordinated FCP for a child with ASD should include:

- **Health Services** Therapy services including speech and language, therapy occupational therapy, physiotherapy and psycho-therapeutic services are generally accessed through Health i.e. Community Child Health, CAMHS and/or Community Learning Disability (CLD) teams. Work should be co-ordinated within the FCP.

- **Social Services** Contact details should be given to families and key worker and advice about benefits and access to local facilities for children including those identified for children with special needs, disability and/or ASD. These might include family support services, both mainstream and specialist childcare; respite services, other leisure and recreational facilities, and short breaks away from home. Therapy services are sometime provided by integrated children's services through the local authority.

- **Local Education Authority** and SEN Parent Partnership Service. Contact details and information about mainstream provision and support, ASD early years and school age provision (mainstream and special), information about *SEN Code of Practice* should be provided.

- **Voluntary sector** Contact details of co-ordinator for local parent support groups, such as local branches of The National Autistic Society, local Autistic Societies, Contact a Family or other local independent initiatives should be given to parents/carers and key worker.

4.3.2   **Specific interventions** (see Appendix A(iv) p91 for more information)

If an ASD is identified then the co-ordinated programme should be ASD specific in terms of its planning but not necessarily its execution. All interventions must be informed by an understanding of ASD, any associated difficulties such as sensory needs, behavioural or mental health problems and how these will affect the particular child. Many parents will have no awareness of the level of ASD training and specialist knowledge available in their local area. Currently this lack of information reduces confidence (English and Essex, 2001).

4.3.2.1   **Family support, therapeutic interventions and information**

Families have to take on multiple roles when their child has an ASD, including the roles of co-therapists and advocates (Schopler and Reichler, 1971). The involvement of families in any therapeutic intervention is crucial. Helping them to develop ways of fostering social-communicative interactions with their child is viewed as particularly helpful. Teaching parents and, where possible other family members to understand and communicate more successfully with their child may also enhance parental and family self-esteem and their ability to cope.

All families should be informed about local training opportunities and interventions. This may take the form of a group training approach such as 'More than Words' (Sowter et al, 2002) where definite diagnosis of ASD is not required; EarlyBird and *help!* (Shields, 2001; NAS 1999): diagnosis of autism/ASD is required for both these NAS initiatives (see Appendix A(iv) pp91). Other initiatives might include individual professional/parent led home based training (such as Portage and any available Visiting Teacher programmes).

Within 4 weeks of the ASD diagnosis, families should receive information about local services and treatment approaches from a knowledgeable professional.

Building on existing knowledge about successful working with children in the home and other settings (Howlin and Rutter, 1987; Schopler et al, 1990), the treatment programmes, for both parents and professionals that seem to be most widely effective at this stage are those that:

- use predictability, routine and consistency as important elements in the teaching of new skills and reducing problem behaviours
- make use of visual strategies to emphasise meaning
- offer small group social opportunities for children and their families
- teach an understanding of the role played by the fundamental deficits in autism in both causing and maintaining behavioural problems
- employ a functional approach to problem behaviours
- build on basic behavioural strategies such as prompting and shaping techniques, to develop more complex skills and the systematic breakdown of complex tasks into their component but meaningful tasks to enhance learning
- use naturally occurring reinforcers (i.e. resulting from the successful completion of the task itself, or using the child's special or obsessive interest).

Very early interventions that assist families to develop appropriate management strategies in the infant/pre-school years and increase social-communication skills for the child and family may well prevent the development of secondary behavioural problems. (Runco and Schreibman, 1987). However, severe behavioural problems will require specific interventions and it is important that families begin treatments early. The specific service identified to provide the appropriate intervention and the details of the intervention should be agreed with the family, supported by the key worker and included in the FCP. The outcome of the intervention must be reported in the annual review of the FCP. Positive behaviour support systems (PBS – see Carr et al, 1999, for review) focus on positive aspects of both the child's behaviour and environment so that appropriate, rather than problem, behaviours can be encouraged (Weiss, 2002). It is important that behaviour problems are not seen as separate from the needs of the child as a whole. This may lead to an unhelpful focus in the intervention plan on behaviour reduction without looking at the preventative value of building up skills (especially communication skills) and understanding to reduce the stress and frustration that may be causing the behaviour.

Parents/carers may also require information about other local services to meet their own adult needs e.g. psychiatric support or individual counselling. Such requests should be co-ordinated through the parents' own general practitioner. Parents also need to be able to spend time with other children in the family (Celiberti and Harris, 1993) and will need to support each other (Bristol et al, 1988).

Other family members (particularly siblings and grandparents) There is increasing awareness about both the needs of other family members and the central role they can play in the family's adaptation through practical and emotional support (Seligman and Darling, 1997).

Local parent support groups
If there are local support groups available then telephone contact or home visit should be offered by the local group co-ordinator.

4.3.2.2   **Child focused interventions** (See Appendix A(iv) p91. See also *Autism: the International Journal of Research and Practice* issues 5:4 and 6:1)
There are a number of different models of intervention programmes for pre-school and school aged children with ASD (Handleman and Harris, 2000), with many features in common (Howlin, 1998; Rogers, 1998; Jordan et al, 1998; Hurth et al, 1999).

It was clear to the working party that good practice exists already in some local areas. **For pre-school children** all local area services should have a trained professional skilled in ASD who can set up a developmental/communication/social and cognitive Individual Education Plan (IEP) at home/nursery for each child and family within 6 weeks of diagnosis, in conjunction with parents and/or the professional responsible for implementing the plan. The IEP should have time-referenced outcomes, be regularly reviewed, and should be clearly referenced to the child's statement of special educational needs, where that exists.

For primary school aged children each local area service should have an educational resource/specialist teacher who can contact the parents and visit a child in school within 6 weeks of diagnosis. This individual must possess the skills to support autism specific educational needs in a range of settings and should contribute to the IEP.

Pre-school education opportunities
The educational programmes that have tended to prove most effective for young children with autism are those that:
• take account of the characteristic behavioural patterns of children with autism, and an understanding of what may underlie those behaviours,
• employ a structured, approach to teaching
• focus on the development of specific skills, and on increasing social communication and understanding (Marcus et al, 2000)
• foster integration with peers.

The optimum length of such programmes is uncertain but there is some evidence that access to 'autism specific' programmes of this kind for around **15 hours a week** with specifically trained staff/workers is likely to result in more enduring gains than much briefer, or non-autism specific forms of intervention (Rogers, 1998). These fifteen hours of specific interventions with an experienced worker could be undertaken either at home or in a nursery. The Working Group is aware that from April 2004, all 3 and 4 year olds will be entitled to government funded nursery/early education placement of 12 $\frac{1}{2}$ hours per week. Fifteen hours of specialist input will have significant training and resource implications for all local areas.

There is a substantial number of studies showing the value of learning amongst one's peers (Lord and MacGill-Evans, 1995; Strain and Hoyson, 2000). However, there is no evidence that placing all children with ASD in mainstream nursery or school settings, without adequate support and structure will lead to positive gains. Indeed, there is some evidence that it may be detrimental and lead to further social withdrawal. Careful analysis of each child's unique needs and the characteristics of the setting should be taken into account when placement decisions are made.

The strategies employed to enable the child to progress should be recorded within an Individual Educational Plan (IEP) which is kept under regular review. The child's specific programme should be designed to:

- develop more effective communication skills (both verbal and non-verbal). This can result in a significant decline in behaviour problems, as well as a marked increase in communication skills
- enhance social interaction – in this age group *adult directed* involvement with socially able peers seems to be particularly valuable
- offer direct teaching of communication, social understanding and play skills
- teach daily life skills, including feeding, exercise and toileting.

Educational interventions for primary school aged children
(With and without defined learning disability) The features associated with identified good practice in ASD are described in Appendix A(iv) p91.

Once a child has received an ASD diagnosis all educational and community staff working with that child and family need to develop an awareness of the child's specific strengths and difficulties. In some districts children have a special book or 'passport card' identifying their personal profile (Pike 2001; English, 2002). The MAA local team and therapists providing general (4.3.1) and specific (4.3.2.) interventions should liaise closely with parents, teachers, educational support staff and specialist educational advisors to develop the IEP. The FCP and Individual Educational Plans need to include clear strategies for all staff to use. These plans should be reviewed at least once a year or more frequently as required.

In school, staff should be encouraged to use an observation profile format to identify the child's particular areas of need. Whilst there is no evidence on which to base specific recommendations, the 'Observation Profile' developed by Cumine, Leach and Stevenson (1998; 2000) provides a good framework for children in mainstream education, whether or not they have additional learning difficulties. When schools are deciding on provision at School Action and School Action Plus under the SEN code of practice and providing advice to the LEA for children who are being assessed for statements of SEN, it would be helpful to include any results from a framework such as an observation profile that may have been undertaken. The guidelines of Jordan and Jones (1999) for mainstream children and Jordan (2001) for children who also have severe learning difficulties provide valuable additional information.

Recommended

- Access to appropriate teaching aids with particular attention to the less structured times within the school/educational timetable (such as break and lunch times).
- Whole school awareness, training and planning for children with ASD.
- Awareness of the motor, perceptual, sensory, daily living skills/self-care, play and leisure needs of the child.
- The emotional needs and reactions of the child must be considered.
- Planned additional individual and small group social skills opportunities tailored to the needs of the child (including supported after school and leisure social clubs).
- Facilitatory learning environments including some form of structured teaching.
- Continued emphasis on communication regardless of spoken language ability.
- Functional and positive support for behaviour.
- Ongoing liaison between school, parents/ carers and community based professionals to ensure consistency of approaches in home, school and any other environment for the child.
- If the child's needs are such that they require a support assistant then the support assistant should receive training in ASD and have some employment security that enables them to develop their expertise and provide an ongoing resource to the LEA/EA.

4.3.2.3   **ASD specific therapies and 'other treatment' interventions** (see Appendix A(iv) p87)

- There is a range of therapies promoted for individuals with ASD. However most of these lack experimental evidence of effectiveness (Smith 1999; Howlin and Charman, in press; Diggle, McConachie and Randle, 2002).

- Scientific evidence of efficacy assumes a homogeneous population. Since children with ASD present as a heterogeneous group it remains possible that some treatments that do not have demonstrated effectiveness across the population, may, nevertheless, be highly efficacious in a small sub-set of that population. Thus, if there is some a priori rationale for using a specific treatment with a particular child, this should be carefully monitored. Single subject case designs should be utilised to assess efficacy and monitor side-effects. Future research initiatives should include published summated case studies. These may provide evidence of more general effectiveness and, given sufficient individual detail, might lead to the identification of treatment-sensitive sub-groups.

- Parents who wish to explore specific 'alternative' therapies for their child should do so with the support and knowledge of their named senior clinician from the base service and their named key worker. Any additional assessments and interventions can then be negotiated with the local ASD co-ordinating group. The child should remain on the Special Needs register and the annual review of the Family Care Plan should also continue so that all agencies remain aware of the needs of the child.

- There is very little evidence that any treatment alters the core symptomatology of ASD (du-Verglas, Banks, and Guyer, 1988; Chez, 2000), although claims such as for the use of naltrexone (Campbell, 1996) or diet (Knivsberg et al, 1998) have been made. There are anecdotal reports suggesting that certain interventions, such as vitamin or psychopharmacological treatments, may benefit some children, and yet they may be entirely unhelpful for others. For these reasons no definite recommendations can be made about individual therapies. There is also emerging evidence that some therapies previously advocated by professionals and parents, such as auditory integration therapy are no more effective than placebo (Mudford et al, 2000; Dawson and Watling 2000), whilst others (such as Facilitated Communication) are now discouraged because of adverse side effects or other risks to the child (Bebko, Perry and Byson, 1996; Dunn-Geier et al, 2000; Campbell et al, 1990; Pfeiffer et al, 1995).

- There is a place for the use of medication in the management of certain co-morbidities, such as epilepsy, anxiety, obsessive-compulsive disorder (OCD) or depression, or as part of a co-ordinated approach to behavioural disturbance (Gringras, 2000; Santosh and Baird, 1999). Medication should be an adjunct to the behavioural and educational interventions within the multi modal FCP. There are limited data on the short term and long term effects of the use of certain medications. There are recent reports of promising trials with the newer neuroleptics and atypical antipsychotic medication (McDougle et al, 1998) and use of selective serotonin reuptake inhibitors (SSRI) (McDougle et al, 1996; Fatemi et al, 1998; Lord and Bailey, 2002). Specialist advice should be sought from the local area lead clinician (CAMHS/LDS) with ASD expertise and links with tertiary services (see 4.4 and 4.5).

4.3.2.4   Ongoing needs

- **Specific developmental disorders** Some children with co-morbid specific developmental disorders will require additional therapeutic services to provide specialist advice to parents/carers and all staff working directly with the child across all settings and/or specialist individual therapy for the child. These services include speech and language therapy for augmented communication programmes, physiotherapy and occupational therapy for visual perceptual problems, fine and gross motor co-ordination difficulties including with writing, unusual sensory responses, self-care skills and provision of equipment and environmental adaptations.

- **Behaviour and mental health problems** Additional and ongoing problems of behaviours and /or learning are common in ASD. Local area services need to be able to provide both continuity of care and reassessment as circumstances change and concerns arise. The services also need to be able to provide appropriate interventions and liaise with all members of the local multi-agency team working in all settings and with the child or family separately and together. Specialist CAMH services (psychiatry, psychology, a range of psychotherapeutic services, nursing, occupational therapy and social work) with a knowledge of ASD are required in every local area. Management of behavioural and mental health problems in conjunction with social-communication needs should be preventative and should be priorities for provision. The working party are aware of the significant training and funding implications required to resource this recommendation. For a small group of children, in-patient CAMHS facilities may be required. Commissioners for children's services need to plan for these facilities to be available for children with ASD and defined learning disability as well as those without LD (see Tertiary Services 4.5).

- **Short break respite services** with specific ASD knowledge may be needed. Some children need a 24 hour placement in an environment that is structured, predictable and supports the optimum function of the child in communication, personal independence and safe leisure skills. Each local area should know how many children at what ages will have need of such services and work collaboratively with neighbouring local areas to make such provision. It is possible that timely and more effective early support and appropriate management of children with ASD may reduce the need for full time 24 hour placements of some young children with ASD.

- For the ongoing and acute medical and dental needs of some children with associated complex medical conditions, the involvement of secondary and tertiary clinical services including neurology, gastroenterology, or other services may be needed both for investigations and management e.g. ASD with complex epilepsy, cerebral palsy, rare syndromes, particular behavioural phenotypes and any acute illness. This may mean access to wards and day case units etc. ASD specific training will be needed for the staff and usually increased levels of staffing is required for this client group. In the same way some children with significant complex needs, such as behaviour difficulties, but without recognised associated conditions may also require specialist dental and/or medical care (e.g. LD team/community dental practitioners).

4.4 Local area ASD co-ordinating group

Most local areas have already created some form of ASD planning or special interest group in response to the growing awareness of the needs of children with ASD and the level of demand for services in their local area.

Recommendation
- **Each local area should develop a multi-agency co-ordinating group that will oversee the development of local area ASD services.**

- The group will be made up of representatives from local parent and voluntary services and the key services that provide multi-agency assessments (MAAs), ASD interventions and support services.

- **Membership** should include:
  Representatives from local parent and voluntary services
  Strategic managers from Health, Education and Social Services
  The named senior clinicians (or representative for) from the Health 'local area base services':
  Primary Care Trust Lead
  Lead child health clinician with special expertise in ASD and child development service service manager of special needs register
  Lead clinician with special expertise in ASD Child and Adolescent Mental Health Services (CAMHS)
  Lead clinician with special expertise in ASD, community learning disability services (CLDS)
  Speech and language therapist with ASD expertise
  Occupational therapist with ASD expertise
  Educational psychologist and/or LEA SEN officer with ASD expertise
  Clinical psychologist with ASD expertise
  Specialist teacher with ASD expertise
  Representative of therapeutic services with ASD expertise (e.g. psychotherapy, music therapy)
  Liaison health visitor
  ASD support worker and/or Social Services representative
  Administrative co-ordinator.

The **responsibilities** of the group include:

1 Liaison with and advice to local commissioning agencies.

2 Local area **training** in ASD for all local community groups. The quality of the training should be monitored and/or externally validated and the training should meet agreed standards for different types and levels of training as set by national negotiation (see Training 4.6).

3 Maintenance and supervision of the ASD **database** and special needs register.

4 **Auditing** effectiveness of local identification, diagnosis and intervention services.

5 **Co-ordination of service planning** and new developments informed by 'local' clinical need.

6 Supporting provision of funding for, and access to, **tertiary clinical services** and establishing close links with specialist services to meet tertiary clinical needs.

7 Co-ordination of academic and training links with a **regional network** to ensure that new developments inform local area practice. This is required at all levels – from community-wide ASD awareness to the specific diagnostic assessment practices employed and the portfolio of intervention expertise required within the local area.

8 The development and planning of **specific support/intervention services** within both specialist and mainstream settings on a local or regional basis.

4.5 Tertiary services *(Stage 3)*

Each local area must have links with a Specialist Tertiary ASD team. In some local areas the Tertiary service may include members of or comprise the local Stage 2 MAA. In other local areas the referral pathway to the tertiary service and the links with the regional ASD academic centre will be negotiated and overseen by the local ASD coordinating group.

Indications for tertiary referral (stage 3)

Tertiary referrals should be made on behalf of the MAA team in response to the following:
• parental request for a second opinion
• persisting doubt about the diagnosis
• complexity of diagnosis, e.g. co-morbidity; family psychopathology
• need for further specialist advice or intervention, e.g. Tier 4 CAMHS, specialist expertise in psychopharmacology
• need for access to other specialist opinions and interventions, such as genetics, paediatric gastroenterology, paediatric neurology, immunology (as before, this list is not exhaustive); this should be negotiated as part of the tertiary assessment plan
• specific need for specialist advice at key transition stages, e.g. secondary transfer.

4.5.1 Specialist advice (in the form of an expert opinion/consultation) should be available (by negotiated contract) without the need to refer the child for a diagnostic re-evaluation/second opinion. Assessment should be undertaken by a multi-disciplinary team with specific clinical ASD training. The staff will usually have a designated special clinical/academic interest in the diagnosis and treatment interventions for pre-school and school aged children with ASD.

Stage 3 tertiary team should provide access to:

- a neurodevelopmental paediatrician and/or child psychiatrist with specific expertise in ASD
- a specialist psychologist (educational/ clinical)
- a specialist speech and language therapist
- a specialist teacher
- a specialist occupational therapist and
- other therapeutic assessments and interventions such as physiotherapy, psychotherapy service (such as child psychotherapy, art, drama, music therapy)
- a specialist social worker
- specialist day and in-patient facilities for assessment/management within CAMHS service – for children with and without defined learning disability – the need for this should be audited across local areas.

4.5.2 Referral process

- The tertiary team should have access to reports of all previous assessments, investigations and interventions used to avoid repetition, prior to undertaking any additional diagnostic assessments.

- The planned use of a tertiary assessment/intervention service should, as far as is practicable, be negotiated with the family and referring local area team involved in the Family Care Plan, to ensure that the new assessments and interventions complement the local ongoing management plans for the child and family. If the child is school-aged then it is essential that the tertiary team co-ordinate with the LEA when considering plans for intervention.

4.5.3 Stage 3 assessment

The tertiary assessment will be planned around the specific question asked and this is often a reflection of complexity/parental wish for second opinion/specific new line management advice including psychological and pharmacological interventions. Assessment should consist of the following:

- **Specialist developmental history** using a standardised diagnostic assessment tool such as the ADI-R or DISCO or equivalent (as new assessment procedures are developed and rigorously evaluated).

- **Additional individual observations** and **investigations** to complement initial local area ASD **diagnostic investigations**. These might include further cognitive assessment, speech and language therapy, occupational therapy, physiotherapy or any other therapeutic assessment procedures required for that individual child. Additional assessments, as part of a research/training protocol, with the consent of the young person (as appropriate) and/or responsible adults, may also be considered.

- **Additional medical investigations** should complement the Stage 2 work up and will be dictated by clinical need (see above) unless specific consent has been obtained to undertake specified research investigations.

- **Assessments** may take place across different settings to investigate situation specific features and degree of pervasiveness of particular behaviours.

4.5.4 The **outcomes** of a tertiary referral will usually take the form of:
- A diagnostic formulation report with proposals for future intervention and support. As with local area diagnostic formulation reports, a tertiary service report should initially be given to the parents for revision of any errors of factual content. The revised report (dated and signed) should, with the parents' agreement, then be circulated to the referrer, the General Practitioner/primary care team and be available to all other professionals working with the child and family.

- A further contact with the referring agency to discuss the implications of the diagnostic formulation. Parents may wish to bring other local support to the follow-up meeting. This process for a follow up contract should be included in the costings of the tertiary opinion.

- Alternatively, the follow up appointment may take the form of a local multi-agency consultation meeting with representative(s) from the tertiary service in attendance, to consider the implications of the tertiary opinion.

- Specialist intervention that may not be available in the local area may be negotiated if appropriate for a particular child and family. Specific treatments and interventions should be carefully co-ordinated with the local multi-agency team supporting the child and family.

4.5.5   **Timeframe**

The waiting time for a tertiary referral should not exceed 3-6 months initially (in line with the NHS Plan Modernisation Targets) and the tertiary assessment process should be completed within 6-8 weeks, unless additional investigations or a period of specific treatment or admission to a day or in-patient service is negotiated.

4.5.6   **Local network**

The tertiary service should provide the link for each referring area, via their local ASD co-ordinating group, to both the tertiary service and in turn a regional 'network'. Ideally the tertiary service should be part of a nation wide ASD network. This type of national network should facilitate the dissemination of new information about evidence based clinical practice, research and training initiatives (see Training 4.6 and Appendix A(v/vi/vii) p96).

4.5.7   **Regional and national ASD networks**

The tertiary service will be expected to provide an academic centre for ASD research and a resource for up to date information about national and international ASD academic and research developments.

4.5.8   **Funding and resource implications**

The aim should be a seamless service efficiently and conveniently delivered to families to their satisfaction and in a way that promotes best practice. This may mean that the tertiary team should work in an advisory role either directly in local areas or through teaching and telephone/e-mail consultation. Funding for tertiary services is currently based on face to face patient contact and mitigates against development of interactive collaborations appropriate for differing and developing professional needs in different parts of the UK. Strategic planning/methods of joint funding across existing statutory agencies should be developed to fund tertiary services appropriate to local needs.

4.6   Training

"It is generally accepted that training is the key to the successful placement of children and young people with autistic spectrum disorders (ASDs). An excellent teacher or support assistant with no formal, specialist training may be able to work with a pupil with an ASD but to really understand how that pupil thinks and learns, they will need a sound background knowledge of autism. Teachers and Learning Support Assistants (LSAs) need to know how to develop pupils' communication, interaction and flexible thinking/behaviour and to also understand why they are working in a particular way with an individual child. In addition, other members of staff (administration, mid-day supervisors and drivers and escorts) need a general level of awareness of ASDs to enable them to respond appropriately to individual pupils."

West Midlands SEN Regional Partnership, 2001

4.6.1   **Locally available ASD training** (including distance learning) is a requirement for all those who come into daily contact with children with ASD including parents/carers, adults, early educators, teachers and all support staff.

4.6.1.1   **Parents/carers and families** (including professional carers such as shared care, foster care, specialist short break and residential care). Training for families must be on-going as individual needs change according to age and circumstances (English and Essex, 2001). All authorities should offer a variety of training courses for parents/carers in the understanding and management of ASD and any additional behavioural difficulties. This training should be delivered by a multi-agency team. Early parent led interventions implementing strategies such as those utilised in 'More than Words' or EarlyBird should be available in all local areas. Follow up parent training initiatives need to be promoted for parents/carers. Readiness for 'training' in a newly diagnosed family needs to be sensitively handled and the variability of need over time constantly evaluated.

4.6.1.2   **Professionals** This report places a heavy emphasis on three levels of specific autism spectrum disorders training within a local area:

1 Training in increasing awareness of ASD is needed for all community based staff.
2 Specific skills in the diagnostic assessment of ASD and related disorders is required for all professionals involved in Stage 2 Multi-Agency Diagnostic Assessment.
3 Specific skills and enhanced understanding for all professionals involved in the delivery of intervention, education and support services for children with suspected ASD and their families.

With the increased ASD awareness and demand for services and for training, many local area services are already developing local training initiatives to meet local professional needs. Some of this training is single agency/disciplinary and some multi-agency, and includes parents/carers. There are a number of examples of good and innovative training in different parts of the UK. (www.dfes.gov.uk/sen, *ASD Good Practice Guidance*).

• Opportunities to access training on a flexible local basis for parents and professionals need to be identified e.g. distance learning, video and on-line training. 'Quality time' (i.e. during working hours) should be identified to deliver training courses in addition to the reliance on 'twilight hours' for training courses.

The presentation and needs of children with ASD are diverse. No one-off training package focusing on a single approach or intervention will be able to meet the training needs of any professional group.

- All local area provisions should keep a database of the ASD knowledge and experience of the staff. This information would increase parental confidence in local provision.

- All local areas should develop a multi-agency rolling programme of initial ASD awareness raising together with specific locally run (or locally delivered, distance) accredited courses. Such training could be co-ordinated with neighbouring local areas as part of a Regional Education Development network. These training collaborations would provide a model for joint training initiatives and promote high quality multi-agency working (English and Essex, 2001).

- This report highlights the need for co-ordination and collaboration between all agencies contributing to assessments, interventions and the regular review of children with ASD and their families. The working group endorse the work and recommendations of the West Midlands SEN Regional Partnership (see Appendix A(v) p96 and English and Essex, 2001).

- This report recommends a mechanism for the co-ordination of ASD services, ongoing training and development of new funded initiatives for the Local Health Community in collaboration with other local area agencies and professional groups through the ASD co-ordinating group. The ASD co-ordinating group also provides the mechanism for the local population units access to tertiary services.

4.6.2 Strategic Health Authority ASD network: training and academic developments

"A regional policy on training that links into multi-agency planning needs to be devised. The policy should have a clear structure that will provide a comprehensive means of identifying local training needs beginning with elected members through to highly specialist personnel in health and education."

West Midlands SEN Regional Partnership, 2001

- Within any strategic health authority area there may be some but not all local areas with the expertise to deliver high quality in-house training and other local areas without the necessary specialism.

- Policies on training that link together multi-agency planning need to be developed. This should be developed on a local population basis. Prior to the recent NHS reorganisation (2001), a model had been proposed by the West Midlands SEN Partnership to meet the identified major training needs. The Partnership suggested two related solutions: 1) each 'region' should appoint a 'region' wide teacher/early educator with responsibility for co-ordinating ASD training across the 'region', and 2) Regional Health Authorities in conjunction with Education, Social Services and the voluntary sector should develop a **forum for regional education development** (FRED).

- Such fora may in turn provide the basis for a national UK network for ASD research and training.

- The development of a national network of the new Strategic Health Authorities provides an opportunity for the training needs of professionals at local area, across a 'region' and for the UK as a whole, to be reviewed.

- There is a need to review the funding of Stage 3 tertiary clinical and research/evaluation services for children, young people and their families with ASD recognising that funding needs to be made available for training/advice and consultation that does not necessarily involve face to face assessment of a referred child. The NIASA Working Group strongly recommend that this is considered by the National Service Framework for children taskforce.

- Finally, there is a need to establish a national multi-agency group to agree and monitor National Standards for training programmes for all levels of ASD training. The NIASA Working Group is aware that the Teacher Training Agency (TTA) has provided National SEN Specialist Standards as an audit tool to help identify specific training and development needs including those for SENCOs (TTA, 1999).

4.6.3   **Professional groups: specific training requirements**

Working group members (excluding lay members, NAS representatives and those with observer status) were asked to briefly summarise the training requirements for professional groups (see Appendix A(v) p96).

- For each professional group some ASD awareness should be incorporated in the core professional training curriculum.

- Evidence of ASD awareness raising training should also be used as a service quality standard in postgraduate continuing professional training. This should be stated in the Children's National Service Framework. Experience of working with children with a complex mix of social communication and behavioural developmental skills and deficits enhances the precision of clinical skills in a number of different areas of practice.

- In each local area at least one staff member of each professional group should receive additional ASD training and develop specific expertise in. ASD. This should include training in currently recommended assessment tools.

- For details for each professional grouping see Appendix A(v) p96.

4.7   **Conclusion**

- *National Autism Plan for Children* provides templates for the range of services required by children with ASD and their families. The plan can be used by interested parties, practitioners, purchasers of services and strategic planners for service developments.

- The Appendices following this report contain further important materials based on the research expertise, clinical and practitioner experience of the Core Working Group and the literature reviews undertaken: this offers users of the report the opportunity to access assessment tools and other essential resource materials. Appendix A evaluates current practice and identifies priorities and strategies for the implementation of much needed research and practice which can lead to better understanding of ASD and which will better inform all working in this field.

- The working group strongly recommends that the Royal Colleges, relevant professional bodies and independent groups lobbying on behalf of adolescents and young adults with ASD convene a representative group to produce a report focusing on the needs of adolescents and adults with ASD. Recent publications (DH, 2001; Powell, 2002) highlight the need for multi-disciplinary, multi-agency co-ordination of resources and opportunities for the majority of adults with ASD. There is an urgent need for such an initiative to propose agreed guidelines for adolescents and young adults with ASD and their families, particularly for transition to secondary schools, school leaving and opportunities for further and higher education.

Appendices

Appendix A

Detailed recommendations
The following materials have all been informed by research and expert advice.

i. **Tables and Figures**

Table 1   Diagnostic criteria for childhood autism (WHO 1993)

Table 2   Time frame for assessment: suggested minimum time frame standards

Table 3   Example of resource costings for assessment

Table 4   Proforma for possible checklist for MAA and intervention planning

Table 5   Example of proforma for ASD developmental history

Figure 1   Flowchart for the identification, assessment and diagnostic process

Table 1

Diagnostic criteria for childhood autism (WHO 1993)

International Classification of Diseases (ICD-10) issued by WHO 1993

A   Abnormal or impaired development is evident before the age of 3 years in at least one of the following areas.

(1) receptive or expressive language as used in social communication;

(2) the development of selective social attachments or of reciprocal social interaction;

(3) functional or symbolic play.

B   A total of at least six symptoms from (1), (2) and (3) must be present, with at least two from (1) and at least one from each of (2) and (3):

(1) Qualitative abnormalities in reciprocal social interaction are manifest in at least two of the following areas:

(a) failure adequately to use eye-to-eye gaze, facial expression, body posture, and gesture to regulate social interaction;

(b) failure to develop (in a manner appropriate to mental age, and despite ample opportunities) peer relationships that involve a mutual sharing of interests, activities and emotions;

(c) lack of socio-emotional reciprocity as shown by an impaired or deviant response to other people's emotions; or lack of modulation of behaviour according to social context; or a weak integration of social, emotional, and communicative behaviours;

(d) lack of spontaneous seeking to share enjoyment, interests, or achievements with other people (e.g. a lack of showing, bringing, or pointing out to other people objects of interest to the individual).

(2) Qualitative abnormalities in communication are manifest in at least one of the following areas:

(a) a delay in, or total lack of, development of spoken language that is not accompanied by an attempt to compensate through the use of gesture or mime as an alternative mode of communication (often preceded by a lack of communicative babbling);

(b) relative failure to initiate or sustain conversational interchange (at whatever level of language skills is present), in which there is reciprocal responsiveness to the communications of the other person;

(c) stereotyped and repetitive use of language or idiosyncratic use of words or phrases;

(d) lack of varied spontaneous make-believe or (when young) social imitative play.

(3) Restricted, repetitive, and stereotyped patterns of behaviour, interests, and activities are manifest in at least one of the following areas:

(a) an encompassing preoccupation with one or more stereotyped and restricted patterns of interest that are abnormal in content or focus: or one or more interests that are abnormal in their intensity and circumscribed nature though not in their content or focus;

(b) apparently compulsive adherence to specific, non-functional routines or rituals;

(c) stereotyped and repetitive motor mannerisms that involve either hand or finger flapping or twisting, or complex whole body movements;

(d) preoccupations with part-objects or non-functional elements of play materials (such as their odour, the feel of their surface, or the noise or vibration that they generate).

C   The clinical picture is not attributable to the other varieties of pervasive developmental disorder

Table 2

Suggested time frame for assessment: minimum time frame standards

STAGE of PROCESS		Response time at each step	Cumulative Time
Referral for general developmental assessment (GDA) (Stage 1 assessment)		6 weeks	
Developmental assessment		7 weeks	
Completion of Stage 1 assessment and report:			
Stage 1 (GDA) Total			13 weeks
If multi-agency assessment (MAA) referral made			
Appointment of key worker within 4 weeks			
Referral to MAA made (Stage 2) Acknowledgment of referral (2 weeks) Personal contact by MAA team member with family and key worker		6 weeks	
Assessment including diagnostic interview		7 Weeks	
Feedback to family		4 weeks	
Stage 2 (MAA)	Total		17 Weeks
Stage 1 and Stage 2	Total		30 Weeks

- The initial assessment at Stage 1 may involve seeing the child over time and at more than one appointment. It may also involve other members of the multi-disciplinary team seeing the child before ASD becomes part of the differential diagnosis. In these circumstances the time scale before referral to Stage 2 may take longer (this is common with higher functioning children and with children under two with severe learning difficulties as well as ASD)

- However if Stage 1 and Stage 2 follow on directly together the process should take about 6-7 months (i.e. 30 weeks)

- Adequate opportunity must be given within the course of GDA and MAA to discuss the assessment findings with the family

- Some district services have established specific nursery placements (NIASA 2002) to assist assessment/observation of children and promote parent training and support examples of good practice.

Table 3 (see over)

Community Health South London NHS Trust
Services for children with social communication disorders
In Lambeth, Southwark and Lewisham

Resources needed to provide the specialist assessment service: Stage 2 MAA (June 2002)

Resource requirements

Funding for specialist services for children with social communication disorder has varied significantly across Lambeth, Southwark and Lewisham. This has led to the differential development of such services across the three Boroughs. We compared working practices in the three boroughs and estimated the current resource allocation. We gathered the best practice together, and estimated the resource consequence. In order to deliver services as set out in this proposal and minimum possible waiting times for specialist assessment the investment required is outlined below.

This proposal includes:

- costings for the full assessment of 60 children per year (more referrals requiring multi-agency assessment would require pro rata increase in resources)
- provision of a limited package of support for families of children newly diagnosed and specialist early intervention for children under 5 (i.e. EarlyBird or equivalent).

This proposal does not include:

- routine follow up of children with ASD (whether by school doctor or psychologist)
- general support and interventions for children with social communication disorders across all the age range from the period post-diagnosis to leaving school and the transition to adult services (including family support worker)
- specialist support and interventions (e.g. behavioural management, psychiatric intervention and psychopharmacology)
- education resources.

The estimate is based on one new child per diagnostic session plus all the work in preparation and after the diagnostic assessment. 60 children per year require approximately 1.5 diagnostic assessments per week (or three new referrals seen every two weeks) to allow for annual leave, study leave, teaching and training commitments.

Tony O'Sullivan, Core Member

Table 3

Example of resource costings for assessment:
Multi-ethnic population in inner city location (June 2002)

Estimated cost of diagnostic and early intervention service for children with ASD and their families (60 referrals per year)[a]

ASD assessment team[b]	WTE	Annual costs (£)(April 2002)
Consultant (paediatrician)	0.90	66,000
Speech and language therapist (SLT)[c]	1.00	41,100
Psychologist	1.00	42,900 [d]
Support worker	0.60	16,000
Administrative support	0.50	10,000
Education: specialist ASD teacher[e]	1.00	34,000
TOTAL	4.80	210,000

(a) Education input is included here. In Lewisham the contribution from the Early Years Service (part of Education) to the EarlyBird course is 2 sessions per week. The course was initiated by committed, EarlyBird-accredited individuals. There are no ring-fenced resources allocated by Education at present.
(b) Mid-points on salary scales are used and employers on-costs are included.
(c) ASD specialist spine points 36-38 £39,565-42,652, including London weighting and on-costs): includes EarlyBird course running twice yearly.
(d) Clinical psychology spine point Sp39 (range 37-39).
(e) Specialist ASD teacher with a managerial role in MAA team.

Figures include London Weighting and employers on-costs
e.g. for whole time equivalent (WTE) SLT inner London +£2,592, outer London +£1,542

Table 4

Proforma for possible checklist for multi-agency assessment (MAA) and intervention planning Management plan for children with autism spectrum disorder

Please check periodically if these actions or services have been discussed or arranged.

Action or referral	Comment	Yes/No	Date
Diagnosis of ASD: has this been discussed with both parents			
Investigations:			
a) Have these been discussed?			
b) Have investigations been carried out?			
c) Has **hearing** been satisfactorily assessed?			
d) Has **vision** been satisfactorily assessed?			
e) **Psychometric measurement:** is this required? (referral to clinical psychology)			
f) Is referral to **occupational therapist** required for **fine motor/ADL** concerns			
Research: consider possible involvement in research (EEG, twin/sibling etc)			
Education:			
a) **Notification** to Education (LEA) (**under 5s**) (1996 Education Act), **cc educ psychology**			
b) Liaison with **educational psychology**			
c) **Pre-school place:** referral to early years service			
d) Referral to special needs adviser, Early Years Service/pre-school specialist resource			
e) Referral to **district portage service**			
Parent training			
Parent course – EarlyBird			
Support:			
a) **Special needs health visitor** and/or liaison with the family HV			
b) Referral to **disability social worker** (assessment: benefits, respite, support etc.)			
c) Behavioural support or counselling: referral to **clinical psychology**			
Information:			
a) NAS information pack			
b) Local parent group-leaflet/access info			
c) Contact a Family leaflet			
Key worker identified?			
Genetic advice: has this been discussed?			
Tertiary referral			
Other			

Lewisham and Southwark checklist (01/11/01)

Table 5

Example of proforma for ASD developmental history

Autism spectrum disorders – an aide-memoire for interviewing parents/carers of young children

This is an aide-memoire-not a formal interview schedule nor a diagnostic tool. The structure and headings are based on the ICD-10 research diagnostic criteria for pervasive developmental disorders. The content draws from the Autism Diagnostic Interview-Revised (Le Couteur, Rutter and Lord, 1994)

Detailed descriptions of behaviours should be elicited through asking open questions. The descriptions will form the basis for judgements to be made by the interviewer. Behaviours need to be judged against the child's developmental level. It is important to clarify the chronology and pattern of development of behaviours.

(Revised by Helen McConachie and Ann Le Couteur, December, 2001 from version created by Paul Bernard, July, 2000)

1   Qualitative abnormalities in reciprocal social interaction

(a) Failure adequately to use eye-to-eye gaze, facial expression, body posture, and gesture to regulate social interaction

Eye-contact
Quantity and quality during communication

Does X look you directly in the face when doing things with you?
Frequency and duration of eye contact?
With a range of people?
Unusual quality?

Facial expression
Range and use of; subtle as well as extreme

Uses normal range of facial expressions? e.g. happy, sad, afraid, embarrassed, surprised, disgusted
Facial expression sometimes inappropriate to the situation?

Social smiling
Spontaneity, range of contexts and people

Smiles as a greeting?
Smiles in response to a smile/a compliment?
Smiles at a variety of people (i.e. not simply parent)?

Gesture
Range and quality

Range? e.g. head shaking, nodding, waving, beckoning, putting out hand to ask for something, shushing
Variety of contexts?

(b) Failure to develop (in a manner appropriate to mental age, and despite ample opportunities) peer relationships that involve a mutual sharing of interests, activities, and emotions.

Interest in other children
Unfamiliar children of same age – interest and interaction with them

What does X think about other children of roughly her/his age whom she/he doesn't know? Is she/he interested? Does she/he try to approach them/interact with them?

Prefers adult company?
Response to other children's approaches
Unfamiliar children of same age – look for efforts to keep interaction going

How does X behave if another child approaches her/him?

Group play with peers
Participation in spontaneous games with other children; attending to peers and modifying behaviour accordingly; flexible and interactive play

How does X play with groups of children (i.e. more than 2 others)?
Can X co-operate in games like hide and seek/ball games?

Peer groups (for older children)

(c) Lack of socio-emotional reciprocity as shown by an impaired or deviant response to other people's emotions; or lack of modulation of behaviour according to social context, or a weak integration of social, emotional and communicative behaviours

Response to other people's emotions

Does X try to comfort you when you are sad/hurt/unwell?
Spontaneity, range of people, quality

Seeks comfort when sad/hurt/unwell?
<u>Unprompted</u> comfort-seeking

Shares in other people's pleasure or excitement? e.g. someone else's birthday

Inappropriate response to another's emotional state? e.g. laughs at another's distress

Greeting behaviour
Response to re-union following everyday separation; look for verbal and non-verbal expression of pleasure

Lack of modulation of behaviour according to social context
Lacks social inhibition because unaware of social cues/social rules

Varies behaviour according to where he is?/who he is with? e.g. in library vs park, with family vs with strangers
Socially inappropriate and embarrassing behaviour?
Over-personal with unfamiliar people?
Socially embarrassing questions/statements? e.g. why are you so fat?

Response to approach by unfamiliar adults
In everyday but non-routine situations

How does she/he respond if talked to by an adult she/he doesn't know? e.g. a friendly lady in a shop

Integration of social and communicative behaviours
E.g. co-ordination of gaze, facial expression, gesture and speech when making social overture

when she/he wants something or wants help, how does she/he try to get your attention?

(d) Lack of spontaneous seeking to share enjoyment, interests or achievements with other people

When pleased/happy – tries to share these feelings?
When interested in something – tries to share the interest with others? When has created something (e.g. drawing etc.) – important to him that others see it? Shares things with others? – unprompted: e.g. food, toys, space on sofa

2 Qualitative abnormalities in communication

(a) A delay in, or total lack of development of spoken language that is not accompanied by an attempt to compensate through the use of gesture or mime as an alternative mode of communication (often preceded by a lack of communicative babbling).

Age when first used single meaningful words (other than mama and dada)? Delayed = after 2nd birthday

Age when first used phrases (2 words, one of which a noun)? Delayed = after 33 months

Pointing to express interest (NB not simply to request)

Does she/he ever spontaneously point at things around her/him? (e.g. helicopter, bus, in distance)

Did she/he ever show you what she/he wanted by taking your hand or wrist? (i.e. use your hand as if it were a tool)

(b) Relative failure to initiate or sustain conversation interchange (at whatever level of language skills is present), in which there is reciprocal responsiveness to the communications of the other person.

Reciprocal conversation (at whatever verbal level possible)
Offering of information and building on other person's response – not limited to conversations about 'special interests'

Can people have conversations with X?
Only about certain topics?
Does she/he add something to what has been said so that the conversation will continue?

Social chat
Just to be friendly – rather than to express needs or give information

'Small talk'?
How often?
With whom?
Asks questions about you (e.g. what you like, think, how you feel)?

(c) Stereotyped and repetitive use of language or idiosyncratic use of words or phrases.

Idiosyncratic use of language
Speech patterns that are clearly odd in content or context; includes self-commentary on own actions. Explore how much it dominates her/his speech

Uses odd phrases?
Speaks in a very formal or precise way – e.g. saying mother instead of mum?
Says the same thing over and over again?
Gives a running commentary on what she/he's doing?

Neologisms
New and obviously peculiar words; not imitated; not metaphors; not part of a game or shared joke

Uses words that she/he seems to have made up her/himself?
Uses words to mean things they don't usually mean?

Delayed echolalia
Repetitive re-runs of things that have been said; out of context; not as part of play or when 'practising' or for re-assurance

Repeats phrases that she/he's heard others say?
Out of appropriate context?

Prosody
Unusual accent, intonation, pitch, volume, rhythm, rate

Anything unusual about the way she/he speaks (e.g. how loud, her/his accent, intonation, speed etc.)?

(d) Lack of varied spontaneous make-believe or social imitative play

Imaginative play
Formation of mental images of things not really present; look for creative and varied use of actions or objects in play to represent child's own ideas; variety, spontaneity and complexity; doll (etc.) as subject as well as object

Plays pretend games? e.g. with cuddly toys, tea sets, action man, cars?
Doll (etc.) as agent of action, as well as actions done to?
Makes up stories within the play? e.g. doll walks to car, gets in, drives to visit someone etc.
Varies from day to day?

Imaginative play with peers
Look for spontaneity, variety, reciprocity, taking lead as well as following

Plays pretend games with others?
What do they do?
Can she/he understand when other children are pretending?

Imitative social play
Look for reciprocal participation as both leader and follower in social games that require imitation and co-ordination of simple actions, e.g. peek a boo, pat a cake, Simon says; also teasing games ('I'm coming to get you') initiating as well as responding

Does she/he play.....?
Does she/he enter into the spirit?
Does she/he spontaneously try to join in?
Just with you or in other contexts too?

Spontaneous imitation of actions
Look for spontaneous imitation of a range of non-taught actions or characteristics; not vocal imitation; not tv/film characters

Imitates people in the family? e.g. pretending to mow the lawn/do the ironing/fix the car

3   Restricted, repetitive and stereotyped patterns of behaviour, interests and activities

(a) An encompassing preoccupation with one or more stereotyped and restricted patterns of interest that are abnormal in content or focus; or one or more interests that are abnormal in their intensity and circumscribed nature though not in their content or focus.

Abnormal content or focus
An interest that is odd or peculiar in itself. Explore how much it interferes with child's/family's life and how much it limits other interests/activities and how much distress if interrupted

Unusual interests? e.g. traffic lights, street signs
Does it interfere with her/his/your life?
How much time does it take up?

For how long has it been an interest?

Abnormal in intensity and circumscribed nature (children aged 3 years and over)
Differs from ordinary hobbies in intensity; usually very circumscribed; non-social; relative non-progression over time; explore how much it interferes with child's/family's life and how much it limits other interests/activities

Any special hobbies or interests?
How strong is the interest?
Does it interfere with her/his/your life?
For long has it been an interest?
Has she/he ever had any objects (other than a soft toy or blanket) that she/he had to carry around?

(b) Apparently compulsive adherence to specific, non-functional routines or rituals

Rituals
Fixed sequences that are performed as if child feels pressured to complete them in a certain way; includes verbal rituals

Has X any rituals (i.e. things she/he seems compelled to do in a certain way)?e.g. touching a certain spot on the wall before going out of the front door? Sequence of words she/he and you have to say?

Difficulties with minor changes in routines
Look for extreme reactions to minor changes in routines of daily life

Upset by minor changes to routines? e.g. having a bath at an earlier time; getting dressed before breakfast rather than after

Difficulties with minor changes in environment
Look for extreme reactions to trivial changes in environment – and efforts made to prevent such changes

Upset by minor changes to surroundings? e.g. how the furniture is arranged, change of car

(c) Stereotyped and repetitive motor mannerisms that involve either hand or finger flapping or twisting, or complex whole body movements

Hand and finger mannerisms
Typically – rapid, voluntary within child's line of vision; not nail biting, hair twisting, nor 'overflow' movements seen in toddlers when excited; distress when interrupted

Any odd ways of moving hands or fingers?
What happens if you try and stop her/him?

Complex whole body movements

Stereotypic, voluntary whole body movements – e.g. spinning; arm waving while on tip-toes; not simple rocking

Any unusual movements of whole body?

(d) Preoccupations with part-objects or non-functional elements of play materials (such as odour, the feel of their surface, or the noise or vibration they generate)

Part-objects

E.g. when playing with car – spins wheels/opens and shuts door

Lines objects up?
Plays with parts of toys rather than the whole toy itself?
Constrains 'normal play'?

Non-functional elements of play materials

Unusually strong interest in sight, smell, taste, texture etc., or strong reactions to sensory experiences

Particularly interested in sight, feel, sound of things?
Strength of interest?
Particularly disturbed by feel, smell, taste?
Are there any sensory experiences (e.g. pain) that she/he seems not to notice?

Undue sensitivity to noise

Is X over-sensitive or show unusual response to everyday noises (e.g. traffic, hoover, hair dryer, toilet flushing)

4   **Age of onset**

(a) How old was X when you first wondered if there might be something not quite right with her/his development?

Below 36 months = significant

(b) Regression

Were you ever concerned that X might have lost skills?
E.g. language? How much language before loss?
E.g. other skills?

5 **Additional behaviours**

(a) Toilet training
Have you started toilet training? Any particular problems? e.g. reluctance to bowel movement.

(b) Eating
Is X a picky eater? Are you concerned about her/his diet?

(c) Sleeping
Do you find it difficult to settle X to sleep/Is this a problem? Does X wake often in the night? Is this a problem?

(d) Aggression
Have there been times when X has been aggressive to other people?
In the family?
Outside the family?

(e) Self injury
Does X ever injure her/himself deliberately? e.g. bites arm, bangs head

(f) Fits/faints
Has X ever fainted or had a fit/seizure/convulsion?

(g) Special skills
Does X have any unusually marked special skills? e.g. shapes, memory, music, drawing

Figure 1: NIASA flowchart of the Identification, Assessment and Diagnostic Process

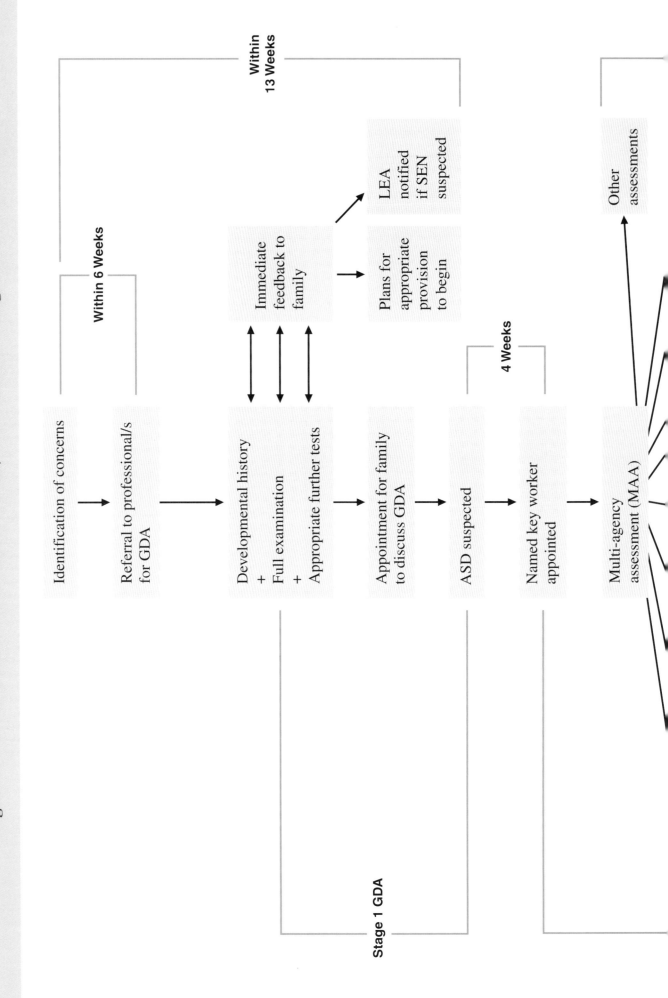

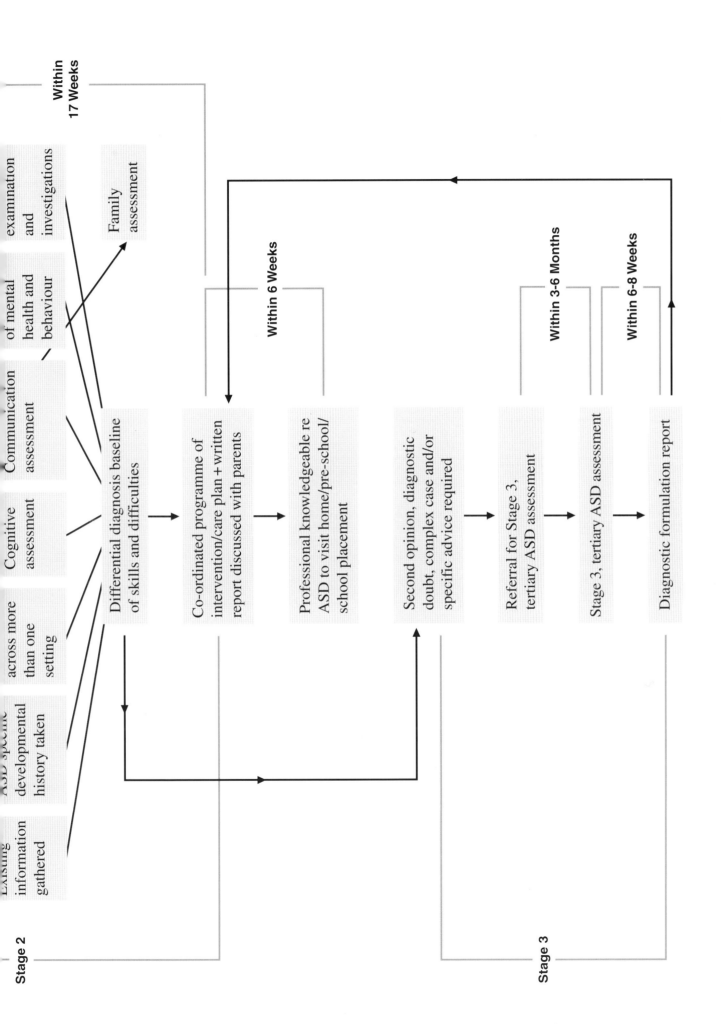

Within 17 Weeks

Stage 2

Existing information gathered

ASD specific developmental history taken

across more than one setting

Cognitive assessment

Communication assessment

of mental health and behaviour

examination and investigations

Family assessment

Differential diagnosis baseline of skills and difficulties

Co-ordinated programme of intervention/care plan + written report discussed with parents

Within 6 Weeks

Professional knowledgeable re ASD to visit home/pre-school/school placement

Second opinion, diagnostic doubt, complex case and/or specific advice required

Referral for Stage 3, tertiary ASD assessment

Within 3-6 Months

Stage 3, tertiary ASD assessment

Diagnostic formulation report

Within 6-8 Weeks

Stage 3

ii.   Identification (see 4.1)

Listed below is a selection of the screening tools mentioned in the report.

Parents Evaluation of Developmental Status (**PEDS**)
Glascoe F. P. MacLean, W. E. and Stone W. L. (1991). The importance of parents' concerns about their child's behavior, *Clinical Pediatrics*, **30**, pp.8-11.

CHecklist for Autism in Toddlers (**CHAT**)
Baron-Cohen et al (2000). Early identification of autism by the *CHecklist for Autism in Toddlers* (CHAT), *Journal of the Royal Society of Medicine*, **93**, pp.521-525.

Baron-Cohen, S., Allen, J., and Gillberg, C. (1992). Can autism be detected at 18 months? The needle, the haystack, and the CHAT, *British Journal of Psychiatry*, **161**, pp.839-843.

Social Communication Questionnaire (**SCQ**)
Previously known as the *Autism Screening Questionnaire* (ASQ)
Rutter et al (2002). *Social Communication Questionnaire* (SCQ). Los Angeles: Western Psychological Services.

Childhood Asperger's Syndrome Test (**CAST**)
Scott et al (2002). Childhood Asperger's Syndrome Test (CAST), *Autism*, **6**, pp.9-31.

Pervasive Developmental Disorder Screening Test (**PDDST**)
Siegel, B. (1998). *Early screening and diagnosis in autism spectrum disorders: The Pervasive Developmental Disorders Screening Test* (PDDST). Paper presented at the NIH State of Science in Autism, Screening and Diagnosis Working Conference, Bethesda, MD.

iii.   Assessment and diagnosis (see 4.2)

Conceptualisation of autism spectrum disorders (see 2.2)
As Frith (1991) has pointed out, the determiners of any 'syndrome' are twofold: firstly, that those with the syndrome should have symptoms in common and secondly, that these symptoms should differentiate them from others. These are the fundamental characteristics of a categorical system of classification on which medical diagnostic systems depend. 'Autism spectrum disorder' (ASD) is not in itself a category within this system, although it broadly coincides with the category of 'pervasive developmental disorder' and includes both 'autism' and 'Asperger syndrome'.

It is a pragmatic category, reflecting the level of knowledge and degree of certainty by which we are currently able to categorise different 'syndromes'. Thus, while it is generally accepted that there are sub-groups within the spectrum, our current divisions are neither scientifically valid nor of practical benefit. It may be the case, however, that there are good social and/or political reasons for some sub-divisions and in the UK at least 'Asperger syndrome' has come to be a shorthand for those within the autism spectrum who have good structural language skills and no general intellectual impairment.

The identification of an ASD is through behavioural 'symptoms', although its biological base is undisputed. The diagnostic systems (DSM IV, APA, 1994; ICD-10, WHO, 1993) currently in use give exemplar behaviours on which a diagnosis may be based. Yet behaviour by itself is a poor guide to diagnosis and certainly there is no single behaviour or even set of behaviours that unequivocally denote autism, although missing behaviours may be a better guide. Making a diagnosis is, therefore, a clinical judgement, with behavioural 'symptoms' as a guide to that judgement. This task is made more problematic by the fact that most behaviours that are seen as 'characteristic' of an ASD can be seen in other (including normally developing) populations, albeit at times of particular stress or in isolation.

A further difficulty for the categorical model of ASD is that the three behavioural domains (communication, social understanding and skill, flexibility in thinking and behaviour) vary dimensionally across both the normally developing and the ASD populations. There is no point (other than an arbitrary one) at which behaviour along any one of these three dimensions can be divided into 'autistic' versus 'non-autistic'. That is why it is always most difficult to make a diagnosis at the extremes of these dimensions where the behaviours merge into mere 'eccentricities' at one end or into severe and profound learning difficulties at the other. It is also the case that many people with ASD view themselves as part of normal human variation, rather than as having a pathology.

The paradox is, that in spite of this failure to differentiate adequately along any one of the dimensions, there are qualitative differences between those who differ on all three dimensions and those who do not, regardless of general ability levels (Wing and Gould, 1979). The two views of ASD can be reconciled by viewing ASD as a broad category sharing certain developmental characteristics within the three dimensions within which there is normal variation, but it is only when someone is situated beyond a certain (necessarily arbitrary) 'cut off' point along all three of these dimensions that they would be categorised as having a disorder. The decision on the 'cut off' point would be a judgement on the extent to which adaptive functioning was affected.

Diagnosis and special needs
The conceptualisation of ASD outlined above sits between a classical medical model of categorisation and an educational model of special needs. There is a consensus that a diagnosis is essential for providing a 'signpost' to needs (Jordan, 1999; Wing, 1996) but there are also dangers in this reliance on diagnosis. Volkmar (1998), for example, has been among those who have pointed out how the use of diagnosis as a gateway to services has distorted the diagnostic process in the US, and the same process can be seen in the UK and elsewhere. A diagnosis can lead to a more valid interpretation of behaviour and identification of needs, but special needs are far from synonymous with a diagnostic category.

The notion of 'special needs' is a relative one, being dependent on both 'within-child' and 'beyond-child' factors. Knowing a child has an ASD directs one to particular hypotheses about the behaviour seen, but that behaviour will also depend on how that child's ASD is affecting the way the child thinks, learns, experiences, and perceives the world and how that interacts with the child's interests, motivation, abilities, memories, experiences, habits and mood. Nor are the influences on the behaviour limited to child factors; behaviour is also affected by the way others are behaving, the way the physical environment is structured, the level of stimulation and so on.

In other words, no matter how pervasive an effect it has on the child's development, the ASD is just one aspect that needs to be considered when determining needs, and the child must be considered as an individual, not as a category. Special needs are not static; they diminish in situations where they are well met and they vary with the child's strengths as well as reflecting impairments.

Rita Jordan, Core Group Member

2[*] ASD specific developmental history

Autistic Diagnostic Interview – Revised ADI-R (WPS)
Lord, C., Rutter, M., and Le Couteur, A. (1994). Autism Diagnostic Interview—Revised: A revised version of a diagnostic interview for caregivers of individuals with possible pervasive developmental disorders, *Journal of Autism and Developmental Disorders*, **24**, pp.659-685.

Le Couteur, A., Lord, C., and Rutter, M. (in press). *The Autism Diagnostic Interview – Revised (ADI-R)*. Los Angeles, CA: Western Psychological Services.

Diagnostic Interview for Social and Communication Disorders (DISCO)
Leekam et al (2002). The Diagnostic Interview for Social and Communication disorders: Algorithms for ICD-10 Childhood Autism, *Journal of Child Psychology and Psychiatry and Allied Disciplines*, **43**, pp.327-342.

Wing et al (2002). The Diagnostic Interview for Social and Communication Disorders: Background, reliability and clinical use, *Journal of Child Psychology and Psychiatry and Allied Disciplines*, **43**(3), pp.307-325.

A number of districts have developed proformas for the developmental history based on ICD-10, DSM-IV Criteria (one example is provided table 5, p64).

3[*] Observational assessment

Assessments which inform needs
The processes of assessment and identification of needs, and diagnosis should be cyclical with each process informing the other. Assessment of needs and diagnosis should be used to develop a profile of the child/young person's strengths and difficulties and inform future planning. Many children with an ASD will require an Individual Education Plan (IEP) which should emphasise teaching learning and thinking skills as well as the social skills that are necessary to function within school and home settings. Education personnel can play a key role in any assessments which inform need. Teachers, specialist support teachers, educational psychologist (EPs) and specialist EPs, learning support assistants, lunch-time supervisors, parents/carers and speech and language therapists can all play a vital role in observing and assessing the child across a range of settings.

Focused observations taken across more than one setting
Observations can provide diagnostic information and help to inform any assessment of needs. Detailed observations and/or video record of the child can be made in their home and in a peer setting (in both unstructured and structured settings). Observations under the headings from the triad will inform both identification and the plan of action.

*Numbers correlate to sequence in 4.2.4.3

- communication
- reciprocal social interaction
- repetitive behaviours.

Other skills it is important to observe are:
- the ability to attend
- to imitate others
- to comprehend and use language
- to play appropriately with toys
- to interact socially with others.

Assessment through teaching

Valuable information about a child's strengths and difficulties and ability to function within pre-school/school/social settings can be gained by assessment through teaching. There are a variety of curriculum – based assessments which can be used together with assessments of the child's learning style. Scaffolding tasks can be used to measure and observe:
- how much input it takes to maintain pupil's attention
- co-operation
- behaviour
- memory
- style of response to task
- response to praise
- situations/activities that appear to generate anxiety
- how much support is needed to communicate response (from assessor and augmentative systems such as PECS or Makaton).

Use of standardised tests

Before any standardised tests are used with children with ASD it should be clear that the information gained will inform future planning. Standardised assessments/tests can, however, be useful as structured observations of learning and response style. As with all children, if standardised tests are used it is important to show the profile of skills; IQ scores can give misleading pictures of a child's abilities. This is especially important when assessing children/young people with an ASD as their profiles are often 'spiky', showing marked strengths and difficulties.

Observation of the environment

It is also important to observe the environment that the child/young person is to operate in. Different settings will require different skills. We need to know what skills the child/young person requires to function in different settings. Does the child have these skills? Are there particular issues regarding the difficulties associated with the triad of impairments?

Dawson and Osterling (1997) identified five important skills that children need to function in the classroom or early years settings:
- the ability to attend
- to imitate others
- to comprehend and use language
- to play appropriately with toys
- to interact socially with others.

It is also important that the child is helped to become as independent as possible in many different settings. Critical elements for independence in the classroom are described by Powers (1992):

- compliance with requests
- turn-taking
- listening to directions form any source
- sitting quietly during activities
- volunteering
- raising a hand to gain attention
- picking up toys/equipment after use
- communicating basic needs
- toiletting.

Observational profile for primary school aged children

There are many commercial checklist and observation schedules that can be used for observing children/young people with an ASD. For example:

Cumine, V., Leach, J., and Stevenson, G. (2000). *Autism in the Early Years: A Practical Guide*. London: David Fulton.

Other examples include in-house observation schedules such as Birmingham's SENCO Questionnaire and Blackpool Learning Support Service's 'Iconic Communication and Interview Observations'.

Annette English, Core Group Member

Checklists are available that provide a framework for characterising behaviours associated with ASD, for example:

Childhood Autism Rating Scale (CARS)

This was initially intended as a screening assessment but is widely used and well known.

DiLalla and Rogers, S. (1994). *Childhood Autism Rating Scale* (CARS); Schopler, E., Reichler, R. J., and Renner, B. R. (1986). *The Childhood Autism Rating Scale (CARS) for Diagnostic Screening and Classification of Autism*. New York: Irvington Publishers.

Vineland Adaptive Behaviour Scales (VABS)

This interview is given to the main caregiver and provides important structured information about developmental level by focusing on everyday skills such as dressing and independent travel.

Sparrow, S., Balla, D., and Cicchetti, D. (1984). *Vineland Adaptive Behaviour Scales*. Circle Pines, Minnesota: American Guidance Service.

Direct observational assessments

Autism Diagnostic Observation Schedule (ADOS)

Lord et al (2000). The Autism Diagnostic Observation Schedule-generic: a standard measure of social and communication deficits associated with the spectrum of autism. *Journal of Autism and Developmental Disorders,* **30(3)**, pp.205-223.

Lord et al (2002). *Autism Diagnostic Observation Schedule (ADOS) Manual*. Los Angeles: Western Psychological Services.

4[*] Cognitive assessment (pre-school and primary school aged children)

Tests used in the cognitive assessment of children with autism

Where they are well standardised, IQ tests are generally considered to be reliable measures of functioning. However there are a number of problems related to the use and scoring IQ tests with young children with autism:

- Very different skills may be assessed by different tests and comparative data are few. Generally the choice of test is determined by tester's familiarity/bias or time/financial costs
- The age range of many IQ tests is limited, so that, especially for longer-term follow-ups, different IQ tests need to be used at different times.
- Scoring protocols for typically developing children may not be appropriate for children with abnormal development, and may result in inaccurate estimates of their level of functioning. Unusual profiles of ability/difficulties, also give rise to problems in establishing basal and ceiling levels.
- Variability in the IQ tests used in different research studies/clinical centres, and lack of consensus on scoring standards can have a considerable impact on how results should be interpreted.

In order to avoid misinterpretation of findings from cognitive tests it is recommended that:

- Rules for scoring of tests when used with children with autism should be made explicit. In particular, decisions on how verbal IQ items are treated (as failures/refusals etc.) in non-verbal children should be made clear. Decisions about reaching basal and ceiling should be clarified.
- Full details of the tests used over time should be presented. Ideally when assessing change over time the same tests should be used. If the original test is not age-appropriate then an additional test should be used as well.
- There should be sharing of information on the relationship between different cognitive tests (i.e. those that tend to give higher or lower cognitive scores).
- Core measures to be used in all outcome studies/comparisons between clinical centres should be agreed.

The following scales/tests are among the most commonly used for the assessment of general cognitive ability (age ranges are given in parenthesis). (See reference list for details of publishers/dates etc.)

- Bayley : 0-42 months
- Mullen : 0-68 months
- WPPSI : 3 years - 7 years 3 months
- WISC : 6-16 years
- Merrill Palmer : 18-78 months
- Ravens CPM 5 to adult
- Leiter 2-18 years
- Vineland 0-adult
- Griffiths 0-5 years
- British Ability Scales (3 levels: 2-3; 3-6; 7-17 years)
- Kaufman-ABC 2-12 years
- McCarthy Scales 2.5 - 8.5 years (also screening test 4-6.5 years)
- Stanford-Binet 2+ years

*Numbers correlate to sequence in 4.2.4.3

No test is without problems and each has various advantages/disadvantages e.g.:

- **Wechsler tests:** WPPSI: Relatively few autistic children within the specified age range are able to complete even the non-verbal items. As they grow older, however, more children seem able to score on the WISC subtests. Both tests provide verbal and non-verbal IQ but scoring leads to problems when children with an IQ below 40 are involved.

- **Merrill-Palmer:** The norms are very elderly (though extended version, 1978 now available). The materials are attractive to children with autism and a test score is often possible to obtain on this when other tests are not successful

- **Bayley:** Assesses verbal and non-verbal skills but it can make a significant difference to scoring if verbal items are coded as omissions or failures (this also applies, but to a lesser extent to the Merrill Palmer). Again, the materials are attractive and work well with children with autism

- **Ravens CPM:** This assesses a restricted range of skills but the book version can be useful for children of lower IQ.

- **Leiter:** Also assesses restricted range of skills; the nature of the sequencing tasks involved may present specific problems for children with autism; however the age range is wide age range wide

- **Kaufman:** Has wide age range; reduced verbal content; attractive materials, and offers analysis of learning styles (eg face recognition)

- **Vineland and Griffiths Scales:** both depend on parental reports; may overestimate observed skills. However, this makes it possible to obtain a score for almost all children

- **Stanford-Binet/ McCarthy Scales:** American only norms; former also has very high verbal content

- **BAS II/ Mullen Scales:** These are relatively new instruments on which more information with regard to use with children with autism is required.

Pat Howlin, Core Group Member

Psychoeducational Profile Revised (PEP-R)
Schopler, E., (1990). *Psychoeducational Profile Revised (PEP-R)*. Austin, Texas: Pro-ed.

Mesibov, G., Schopler, E., and Caison, W., (1989). The adolescent and adult psychoeducational profile: assessment of adolescents and adults with severe developmental handicaps, *Journal of Autism and Developmental Disorders*, **19**, 33-40.

This is a semi-structured observational assessment which can be useful especially for non verbal children. Skills are assessed in 3 different ways: passing, emerging and failing - useful for developing intervention programmes. A long test with 174 items. Poorly standardised. Recommended for use in children age 6-7 years with developmental levels between 2 and 5 years

Jennifer Ravenhill, Educational Psychologist, NAS

5[*]   **Communication, speech and language assessment (pre-school and primary school aged)**

The choice of language assessments will depend on individual factors within the child. Listed below is a range to aid the selection process.

The Autistic Continuum: an Assessment and Intervention Schedule, Aarons, M. and Gittens, T., 1992, Windsor: NFER-Nelson.

British Picture Vocabulary Scale: Second Edition (BPVS: 3-16 years)
1997 Windsor: NFER-Nelson.

Reynell Developmental Language Scales: Third Edition (RDLS 15 months - 7 years)
1997 Windsor: NFER-Nelson.

Derbyshire Language Scheme
1980 Knowles and Masidlover Derbyshire County Council.

Clinical Evaluation of Language Fundamentals (CELF-Preschool 3 - 6.11years)
2000 (UK edition) The Psychological Corporation.

Clinical Evaluation of Language Fundamentals (CELF - 3UK 6 - 21 years)
2000 (UK edition) The Psychological Corporation.

Renfrew Language Scales: Action Picture Test, Word Finding Vocabulary Test, Bus Story Test.
(3 - 9 years)
Bicester Speechmark.

Test of Reception of Grammar (TROG 4 - 12 years)
1983 Bishop University of Manchester

Symbolic Play Test (1 - 3 years)
1988 Windsor: NFER-Nelson.

Test of Pretend Play (ToPP 1 - 6 years)
1997 The Psychological Corporation.

The Pragmatics Profile of Early Communication Skills in Children (9 months - 10 years)
1995 Windsor: NFER-Nelson

The Social Use of Language Programme (SULP Children and Adolescents)
1992 Windsor: NFER-Nelson.

Understanding Ambiguity (8 - 13 years)
1996 Windsor NFER-Nelson

Theory of Mind Stories
In: Happé, F. (1994). *Autism - An Introduction to Psychological Theory*. London: UCL Press.

*Numbers correlate to sequence in 4.2.4.3

Bowler, D. M. and Strom, E. (1998). Elicitation of first-order 'theory of mind' in children with autism, *Autism: the International Journal of Research and Practice*, **2** (1), pp33-44

Maureen Aarons and Tessa Gittens, Core Group Members

6[*] Behavioural and mental health assessment

A specific, systematic assessment of behaviour, temperamental characteristics and current mental state is essential. In some services self report scales, mental health checklists and semi-structured interviews are considered as part of the assessment protocol. There is no evidence base for using currently available mental health diagnostic assessment tools with children with ASD. Indeed caution must be used when considering the reliability of such assessment tools and in the interpretation of clinical meaning for children with ASD.

The assessment must include the diagnosis of ASD, co-morbid developmental disorders and psychiatric disorders. Recent surveys of children and young people with ASD have reported increased rates of psychiatric co-morbidity. Co-morbid mental health problems, such as anxiety, depression, OCD, ADHD/hyperactivity should be identified and treated (Ghaziuddin and Greden, 1998; Gordon et al, 1993)

Most studies have considered older children and adolescents (Green et al, 2001; Gilchrist et al, 2001; Tantum et al, 2001; Howlin, 2000; Hutton et al, in preparation). Recent reports of the use of newer antipsychotic medication and SSRIs; need replication but emphasise the importance of a multi-agency approach to assessment and intervention.

Bromley et al, (2002) conducted a recent postal questionnaire with parents/carers. They reported high rates of emotional disturbance in children aged 3-18 years (caseness criteria was met in 91% of the sample). The behaviours and symptoms identified by parents/carers included disruptive behaviours (52%); anxiety (56%); self absorbed (43%); communication disturbance (40%); anti-social behaviour (48%).

Ann Le Couteur, Core Group Member

7[*] Family assessment

The family is the child's best resource. Indeed parents of young children with ASD have been described as their child's co-therapist since 1970s (Schopler and Reichler, 1971). The *Framework for the Assessment of Children in Need and their Families* (2000) may provide a useful framework for the systematic evaluation of family strengths, parenting styles, capacity and wider family issues.

Extract from: *Framework for the assessment of children in need and their families (2000)*

In April 2000 the DoH issued a national framework for assessing children in need and their families, under Section 7 of the *Local Authority Social Services Act 1970*, which means that it must be followed by Social Services Departments unless there are exceptional reasons not to do so. However, it is also intended to provide a foundation for policy and practice for all professionals and agencies who are responsible for providing services to children in need and their families. Social Services Departments are already working together locally with other agencies, to implement the Assessment Framework model across the agencies.

*Numbers correlate to sequence in 4.2.4.3

The model is based on three domains: The Child's Developmental Needs, Parenting Capacity, and Family and Environmental Factors. Within each domain there are a number of Dimensions, as set out below. The assessment is undertaken in partnership with the child and family, and the analysis of information gained through the assessment process, provides the basis for an interagency plan to help the child and his or her family.

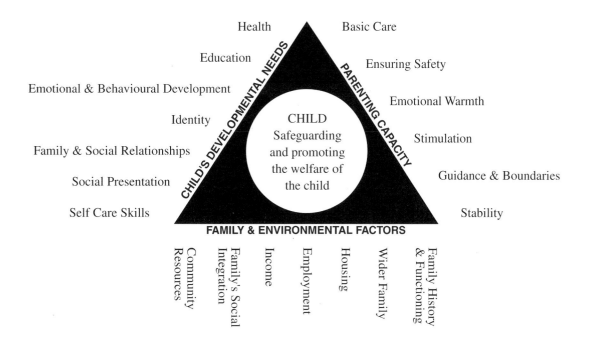

The assessment framework provides a relevant and useful tool for assessing the needs of the children and young people with learning disabilities and mental health problems, giving equal weight to parenting capacity and family and environmental factors, as to the developmental needs of the child.

Many of the stresses experienced by families with a child with ASD are common to families with a child who has a disability but the literature suggests that parents of children with ASD have significant unmet needs. Bromley et al (2002) reported that 93% of parents did not receive help during holidays; 87% requested a break from caring; 81% needed advice on education and 80% identified a need for advice on behaviour. 40% of those parents interviewed described their housing as unsuitable.

Overall 59% of the mothers had significant psychological distress. This level of distress was associated with low levels of support and high levels of challenging behaviour from their child with ASD.

A number of studies have now confirmed an increased risk for both autistic spectrum disorder and a broader range of cognitive and social difficulties in relatives of probands with autism (Bailey et al, 1995; Bolton et al, 1994). Only a small proportion of relatives will show clear cut autism, whilst the majority of affected individuals will have a range of related social difficulties and personality traits that appear to co-occur (Bailey et al, 1998; Szatmari et al, 1998). The broad range of difficulties seem to map onto the domains of impairment in autism in ICD-10 and DSM-IV (namely social interaction, communication and restricted, repetitive behaviour). The third domain (restricted, repetitive behaviours) has received much less investigation when compared with studies of social and/or communication impairment. Repetitive behaviours are certainly more difficult to define and study. In contrast with findings in individuals with autism, recent studies of relatives have shown no clear association with either mental handicap nor a consistent pattern of cognitive discrepancies (Fombonne et al, 1997; Folstein et al, 1999).

Whether for relatives of an affected individual with autism, in addition to the increased genetic susceptibility to ASD and the broader phenotype, there is also a pre-disposition to other psychiatric disorders, is at present unclear. Some family studies of autism and ASD have reported increased rates of psychiatric disorder especially affective disorders (particularly major and recurrent depressive illness) amongst relatives (Bolton et al, 1998). These disorders do not seem to overlap with the autistic-related social or language deficits, either at the individual (Piven and Palmer, 1997) or familial level (Bolton et al, 1998). Further, there are reports that adult relatives also have increased rates of anxiety-related personality traits (Murphy et al, 2000) and anxiety disorders (Smalley et al, 1995; Bolton et al, 1998). There is no consensus about whether the risk is for generalized anxiety disorders or social phobia. Despite the need for further studies to replicate this work, these findings need to be taken into account when undertaking an assessment of family strengths and needs and how best to support families with a child with possible ASD.

Christine Lenehan, Council for Disabled Children
Ann Le Couteur, Core Group Member

8[*]   Physical examination

See chapter entitled 'Physical Examination and Medical Investigations' by Anthony Bailey (2002) in *Child and Adolescent Psychiatry,* 4th edition, (Eds Rutter, M. and Taylor, E., Oxford: Blackwell Publishers).

9[*]   Medical investigations

- **Frequency of known medical conditions associated with autism.**

Gillberg and Coleman (1996): Review of 7 studies investigating children with autism (1979-91). Found 11-37% had known medical conditions, commenting that the positive rate increased with severity of learning disability and extent of investigations.

Fombonne et al (1997): In a population-based study of medical disorders excluding epilepsy reported that medical conditions were recognised in 10% (similar in narrowly defined autism and Pervasive Developmental Disorder (PDD)). Tuberous sclerosis was the only condition more strongly associated with autism than with other developmental disorders. The extent to which the children in this study were investigated was not clear. Fombonne's (1999) review of 23 epidemiological surveys (a total of 4 million subjects, 1500 cases) noted associated medical conditions in 6%.

Barton & Volkmar (1998): Investigating 3 groups (autism, PDD and other developmental disorders) reported that 9.8% of the autism group had strictly defined medical conditions (versus 22% of the other 2 groups). Positive findings were correlated with low IQ and broader spectrum PDD (as defined using DSM-IIIR).

Skjeldal et al (1998): Extensively investigated 25 children with autism and age matched IQ controls. 8% of children with autism versus 36% of the controls had associated medical conditions.

*Numbers correlate to sequence in 4.2.4.3

Practice point: A minority of children with ASD (approximately 10-15%) have known medical conditions and the rate is likely to vary depending upon how extensively the children are investigated (Rutter et al, 1994), and on the severity of their learning disability. However, extensive investigation for conditions that do not have implications for management of the child or genetic counselling are not recommended.

- **Basis of specific medical investigations**

Genetic investigation: Autism is positively associated with certain genetic conditions; for example, 40 - 60% of children with tuberous sclerosis are reported to also have autism (Hunt & Shepherd 1993; Gillberg et al, 1994), and 15-30% of those with Fragile X (Bailey et al 1998; Hagerman et al, 1986). Conversely a much smaller percentage of children with autism will have a specific genetic basis for their condition. For example in a study of tests in children looking for undiagnosed aetiology for autism, 3% had abnormal karyotype including 4 out of 11 with Fragile X (Lewis et al, 1995).

Practice point: Genetic investigation is likely to have higher pick-up if targeted to individual conditions on the basis of a raised index of clinical suspicion.

Imaging studies: Abnormalities have been reported both in the cerebellum and also cortical migration anomalies in some individuals. There are no consistent diagnostic findings in autism.

Practice point: Routine imaging in ASD is not indicated. Imaging in tuberous sclerosis is indicated, because of association of the triad of autism, epilepsy and severe learning disability.

Epilepsy, epileptiform EEGs and autism: Epilepsy is common in autism. Current estimates of the lifetime incidence of epilepsy in autism is 17% (Fombonne, 2001). Epilepsy may arise at any age but two peaks are recognised, in early childhood and adolescence. The probability of epilepsy increases with the severity of the underlying brain dysfunction as shown by the presence motor deficits and mental retardation (Tuchman, 1991). Thus within the population of children diagnosed with ASD there will be many who require the investigation and management of epilepsy.

Regression occurs in a variable number of children with autism, around a mean of 21 months (Tuchman 1996), but the prevalence of epilepsy is not greater in those who show early regression compared with those who do not. In a group of 585 children with autism, 11% of those without regression had epilepsy compared to 12% of those with regression (Tuchman, 1991). Epileptiform EEG's are common in autism and are marginally more prevalent if there is a history of regression. Prolonged sleep EEG monitoring increases the sensitivity of detection of an epileptiform EEG. No child in the Tuchman study had electrical status epilepticus during slow wave sleep (ESES) as would be found in Landau-Kleffner syndrome. Thus the significance of an epileptiform EEG in autism with or without regression remains unclear and the results of treatments are inconclusive. Treatment with anti-epileptic drugs for epileptiform discharges is not without risk, and there is a lack of evidence of effectiveness (Ronen, 2000).

Practice point: Routine EEGs in ASD are not indicated; rather investigation should be based on clinical grounds. Some children who have a fluctuant course of behaviour or other unusual features will need the opinion of a paediatric neurologist but the place of routine EEG monitoring in characteristic autism with a history of loss of use of words within the first 10 word stage, is not recommended. Much later developmental regression with onset of autism following normal development to 24 months or beyond (childhood disintegrative disorder) is rare (7-8%) and is associated with greater regression of all functions. (Volkmar 1994). More extensive neurological investigation may be warranted in this subgroup.

The corollary is that among services for children with epilepsy a significant number of children will need assessment and comprehensive services for ASD. In early onset (under 2 years of age) severe epilepsy, ASD is particularly common, usually combined with severe cognitive impairment, and often attention and hyperactive symptoms and co-ordination impairments. Services for epilepsy and ASD need integration at training and service levels. Children with ASD who have epilepsy should be investigated and managed according to the usual protocols for epilepsy. Children who have epilepsy and associated developmental disorders need the same general and specific assessments recommended in this report for suggested ASD.

Inborn errors of metabolism: In the Fombonne (1999) review phenylketonia (PKU) and other inborn errors of metabolism were causes in less than 1% of cases of autism. Conditions considered to be associated with autism are

1 Phenylketonuria currently screened for at birth
2 Tyrosine hydroxylase deficiency which is accompanied by gross neurology
3 Methylmalonic acidurea in which there is acute decompensation
4 Ornithine transcarbamylase, purine and pyrimidine disorders which are non-specific
5 The mucopolysaccaridoses in which there are dysmorphic features
6 Mitochondrial cytopathies with very wide spectrum of presentation
7 Smith's Lemli-Opitz in which there is dysmorphology.

Practice point: The indications generally for looking for inborn errors of metabolism are mental retardation, encephalopathy, recurrent vomiting and dysmorphic features. Screening for inborn errors in the absence of clinical features which suggest further investigations, cannot be routinely recommended.

Other abnormalities for which there are some available studies:

1 Evidence has been presented for abnormalities of bowel function including increased bowel permeability, antibodies to gluten or the presence or absence of gut permeability in autism. The latter has been found in one study only; antibodies to gluten are not noted to be raised in autism. Evidence for inflammatory bowel disorders (IBD) in autism is still at the investigation/research phase but constipation and variable bowel symptoms are common and one group of researchers have found possible auto-immune complexes (Murch, 2002).
2 Vitamin deficiencies e.g. B12 and yeast overgrowth: evidence for latter is insecure.
3 Low plasma sulphate and increased sulphite, thiosulphate and sulphate ions in the urine (Waring 2001): low plasma sulphate in 92% of children with autism.
4 Excess Indolylacryloylglycine (IAG) in the urine: discussed by Shattock (2001) IAG is said to be increased in the urine of those with autism but it is not clear what the meaning of this is and whether it is specific to autism: further studies needed (Waring, 1993).
5 Research studies of anti neuronal antibodies (for example, antimyelin basic protein) to date have all involved small numbers. The relevance of these findings are difficult to comment on, further research is needed.
6 Lead levels – no new evidence was considered during the NIASA review.

Gillian Baird, Core Group Member
Hilary Cass, Neurodisability Consultant, Great Ormond Street Hospital

10[*] Other assessments

Suggested occupational therapy assessments suitable for Stage 2/Stage 3 assessments

Screen with:
Movement ABC Checklist (Henderson and Sugden, 1992), and/or *Developmental Co-ordination Disorders Questionnaire* (Wilson et al, 2000)
The Sensory Profile (Ermer and Dunn, 1998; Watling et al, 2000)

Assessment instruments:
Movement ABC Test (Henderson and Sugden, 1992)

A Gesture Test (Bergers and Lezine, Kaplan, 1976; Cermak et al, 1982; Njiokiktjien et al, 2000; Green et al, 2002)

A Visual Perceptual/Spatial Assessment (VM1 and supplementary tests or MAT) (Gardner 1988; Naglieri, 1986; Colorusso and Hammill, 1996; Hammill, Pearson and Voress, 1998)

Play Assessment and/or *School Function Assessment* or *School Based Assessment of Motor and Process Skills* (Bundy, 1997; Knox, 1997; Ziviani et al, 2001; Filipek et al, 1999; Coster et al, 1999; Fisher, 1995).

Dido Green, Guy's Hospital

iv. Interventions (See 4.3)

Early interventions for children with ASD (See 4.3)

Summary
A detailed literature review was conducted of a range of different treatments for young children with autism. The focus was on therapeutic interventions of a non-medical kind, although reviews of pharmacological, dietary and other physical treatments were also briefly considered.

The findings generally support the view that early educational/behavioural programmes are a good option for young children with ASD but there is little evidence in support of any one specific methodology, or intensity of treatment. Certain pharmacological treatments also seem to be effective, but further research is required to pinpoint which particular medicines work for which particular children, and for which particular types of problem. There was little or no scientific evidence in support of dietary or vitamin treatments, or the use of secretin. Experimental data in support of a variety of other treatments, such as Facilitated Communication, auditory or sensory integration programmes, psychoanalytically based interventions or teaching methods such as the Son Rise programme (Option), Walden or Daily Life Therapy (Higashi) did not exist. Thus, whilst some of these approaches may be helpful for individual children with ASD and their families, there is no evidence to support their wider use. Moreover, in the case of Facilitated Communication there was some evidence to suggest that it should not be used at all.

In the UK, however, approaches to education at all levels are largely eclectic and case study evidence was provided of centre-based education focusing on communication and social interaction skills as

*Numbers correlate to sequence in 4.2.4.3

well as direct skills teaching. There were also home-based programmes, some of which also had a communication focus or behavioural skills based approach. Good models were presented of early intervention based on parent training either following directly on diagnosis (EarlyBird: Shields, 2000; Nottingham Early Years centre: Christie et al, in press) or from the first confirmation of suspicion (Sowter et al, 2001; Sussman, 1999).

Whilst no one approach to treatment can be recommended for all children with autism, evidence from psychological and educational research more generally can be used to indicate the types of strategies that are most likely to be helpful for this group of children. These are summarised below. Recommendations for evaluating new or existing therapies are also presented.

Current findings
In the field of autism very many different treatments have been suggested as being able to bring about remarkable improvements, or even cures for children suffering from this condition. Therapies as diverse as swimming with dolphins, being swung around in nets, dosing with evening primrose oil or listening to tapes of filtered sound have all been suggested as effective. However, recent reviews have generally indicated that many of these claims are made in the absence of any scientific data (Howlin, 1997; Rogers, 1996; 1998, New York State Department of Health, 2000). 'Evidence' for many of these treatments is based simply on anecdotal reports of successful cases, with little information either on the exact nature of the treatment, or the types of child involved. Rarely is any information presented on the types of children who did not respond.

In the few cases where highly popular interventions have been subject to experimental research, the results have often been far from positive. In the case of Facilitated Communication, for example, extensive experimental studies demonstrate conclusively that this did not result in enhanced independent communication by the children involved (Bebko, Perry and Bryson, 1996). Moreover, because its use has led to unsubstantiated claims of physical or sexual abuse, it is now strongly discouraged (New York State Department of Health, 2000: American Psychological Association, 1994). Auditory integration therapy has also recently been subject to careful analysis, and again the results indicate that the effects are no greater than for placebo conditions (Mudford et al, 2000; Dawson and Watling, 2000).

Whilst dietary and vitamin treatment have their advocates, both amongst professionals (Knivsberg et al, 1995; Reichelt et al, 1991; Shattock et al, 1998) and parents, scientific evidence in support of such interventions is lacking. Anecdotal reports suggest that while these treatments may offer benefits for some children, they are entirely unhelpful for others, and there is no clear criteria for determining which children are likely to show negative or positive effects. It is important to be aware that substantial modifications to a child's dietary or vitamin intake, without appropriate monitoring can have serious physical consequences. In addition, restricting the diet of a child who already has rigid eating habits can lead to an exacerbation of feeding problems.

Pharmacological treatments are used much more widely in the US than in the UK (Gringras, 2000), and although the quality pharmacological research is generally higher than for many other types of interventions (New York State Health Department Review, 2000) large scale randomised control studies of children with autism are still rare. Gringras (2000), reviewing the use of pharmacological treatments for children with ASD in the UK, concludes that much of the early research in this field has generated false hopes. Fenfluramine, for example, previously widely used in the US, has been virtually withdrawn because of adverse side effects; whilst initial control trials of secretin (Sandler et al, 1999; Chez et al, 2000) indicate no advantages over placebo.

One of the most recent, detailed reviews of therapies currently used for children with autism is that of the New York State Health Department (2000). In a systematic review of interventions currently in use in the US, they concluded that the majority of studies did not even meet the basic requirements of describing the treatments or children involved adequately to allow for replication. Of those that did, fewer still met basic criteria for experimental research. For inclusion in the review single case studies could be included if they involved more than three individuals with ASD, and used a standard single subject research design (multiple baseline, ABA etc.). Group studies were included if they compared a treatment vs a no treatment/different treatment group, if subjects were assigned to treatment in ways that did not lead to bias, and if equivalent methods were used for measuring baseline and outcome in both treatment and controls.

Although this review focused almost exclusively on US based treatments, the overall conclusions reflect the findings of other reviews in this area (e.g. Howlin 1998; Rogers 1996). Thus, in the majority of studies the standard of experimental research was poor and evidence for the effectiveness of any one specific treatment was limited. The programmes that seem to be most widely effective are those involving early behavioural interventions (Lord, 2000; Schreibman, 2000). These may follow strict behavioural lines (e.g. the ABA programmes of Lovaas and colleagues: McEachin, Smith and Lovaas, 1993; Smith, Groen and Wynn, 2000) or they may also incorporate broader developmental and educational strategies (e.g. Harris et al, 1991; Rogers 1998). A number of comparative and review studies now indicate clearly that behavioural approaches generally, particularly those that begin in early childhood, do lead to positive improvements in children with autism, both with regard to behavioural problems, the acquisition of new skills and greater social integration.

Nevertheless, there is no evidence in support of one specific approach, degree of intensity, length of intervention, or home vs school based programmes. There is some indication, however, to suggest that very brief treatments are ineffective, and that programmes involving 20 or so hours per week are likely to result in more enduring gains (Rogers, 1998). The involvement of families in therapy also seems to be crucial for generalisation and maintenance (Howlin and Rutter, 1987). For this reason current intervention programmes have begun to focus specifically on helping parents to foster communicative interactions with their child in the months following diagnosis (Shields, 2000; Sowter et al, 2000; Sussman, 1999).

The way forward
Although few of the more sensational claims for treatment have been substantiated by hard evidence, and there are still no good data to indicate that any one particular treatment is the gold standard for all children with autism, more general findings from psychological and educational research are important in indicating what components of a treatment package are likely to be most effective.

Very early studies of educational programmes for children with ASD (Rutter and Bartak, 1973; Lansing and Schopler, 1976) indicated that structured teaching programmes, focusing on the learning of specific skills, resulted in greater progress, both academically, socially, and behaviourally. The term 'structure' refers to the degree to which ambiguity and confusion is removed from the teaching/learning situation. This is done through modifying (often, but not exclusively, through visual means) the physical environment, the instructional medium, time, space and the learning task so that answers to 'what?' 'where?' 'when?' 'for how long?', 'how?' 'what next?' and 'who with?' questions are all immediately apparent to the child, or can be taught to be so. TEACCH (cf Schopler, 1997) is a prime example of this kind of cued learning, although the principles of TEACCH include other aspects such as individualisation and functionalism.

Many other interventions rely on structured teaching although this may involve various different forms eg discrete trial, one to one teaching; interactive interventions based on music and play methods (e.g Christie et al, 1992; Nind and Hewett, 1994), and, more recently cognitive methods, sometimes involving computer assisted learning, designed to teach specific cognitive skills in an attempt to replace external with internal structures. Although there are no evaluations of such programmes in natural settings over the medium to long term, immediate gains are often apparent.

There is a large body of research on the importance of helping children with autism develop more effective communication skills (both verbal and non-verbal). Supplying children with more efficient ways of communicating their needs can result in a significant decline in behaviour problems, as well as a marked increase in communication more generally (Durand and Carr, 1991). The value of non-verbal strategies for increasing communication skills in more severely impaired children is also well documented (Durand, 1990; Koegel 2000; Prizant et al, 1997).

The importance of a functional approach to problem behaviours, and understanding the role that a fundamental deficits in autism (communication, social understanding, and ritualistic and stereotyped behaviours) may play in causing or maintaining behavioural problems has had a major impact on educational and therapeutic strategies (Dawson and Osterling, 1997).

For nursery and pre-school children, in particular, the value of involving peers as therapist has been demonstrated in a number of studies (Lord, 1995; Wolfberg and Schuler, 1993).

Basic behavioural strategies such as prompting and shaping techniques, backward and forward chaining to develop more complex skills and the systematic breakdown of complex tasks into their component tasks have all been demonstrated to enhance learning (Prizant and Rubin, 1997; Koegel and Koegel, 1995; Anderson and Romanczyk, 1999). Whilst the importance or reinforcement has been demonstrated in numerous studies, it now also appears that naturally occurring reinforces (resulting from successful completion of the tasks itself) are likely to be more effective, and result in greater generalisation than extrinsic reinforcers such as sweets.

Predictability and routine, and consistency of management strategies have also been found to be important elements, both in teaching new skills, and reducing problem behaviours (Koegel and Koegel, 1997).

Finally, whilst there have been no studies directly comparing children who receive very early interventions with those for whom intervention begins later, a number of studies have suggested that if appropriate management strategies are developed early on in the children's life, this may well prevent the development of secondary behavioural problems subsequently (e.g. Howlin and Rutter 1978; Institute of Medicine, 2001; Stone et al, 2000; Harris and Handleman, 2000). Programmes involving parents of very young children, in which they are helped to understand and communicate more effectively with their child, also suggest that parental self esteem and ability to cope is enhanced by support in these earliest years (Shields, 2000).

Rita Jordan and Pat Howlin, Core Group Members

General interventions: (see 4.3.1)

Key worker

Person who:

- has specialist knowledge of autistic spectrum disorders
- has dedicated time
- relates to the child and family
- offers liaison
- is able to take an overview
- has the ability to recognise need
- is able to work collaboratively
- is skilled in team working
- recognises that the child is the focus
- is an advocate for the child.

The **key worker** will be part of the team that is involved with the child and family to:

- ensure follow up support, especially in relation to post-diagnosis issues and behaviour management
- ensure guidelines are in place to enable all people involved with the child to work consistently
- recognise when short breaks are necessary and, if necessary, negotiate this
- help parents prepare for children's long term needs
- co-ordinate the transition from children's services to adult services
- co-ordinate service provision and ensure that management plans are followed. (This should include all the child's needs and interventions.)

By permission of the Warwickshire Social Development Team (English, 2002)

Specific interventions (see 4.3.2)

Family support, therapeutic interventions and information (see 4.3.2.1)

Examples of group training approaches

- **EarlyBird**
  Shields, J. (2001). The NAS EarlyBird Programme: partnership with parents in early intervention. *Autism*, **5**, pp.49-56.
- **More than Words**
  Sowter et al (2002); Sussman, F. (1999). *More Than Words: Helping Parents Promote Communication and Social Skills in Children with Autism Spectrum Disorders:* Toronto: Hanen Centre.
- *help!*
  A six session information and support programme for parents/care of school age child, young people and adults with ASD. Email: help!@nas.org.uk

Child focused interventions (See 4.3.2.2)

Educational interventions for primary school aged children

Features that are associated with identified good practice in ASD provision are:

- staff knowledgeable about ASD and able to observe and interpret behaviour in the light of that understanding and resources to liaise with specialist advisors (educational psychologists or advisory teachers) as necessary

- flexibility in school arrangements that permit adaptations to meet needs (e.g. individual working space arrangements, time for transitions, management of participation in assemblies, playtimes etc.)
- commitment to the child and recognition that problems are transactional failures from which all must learn and adapt
- explicit and clear rules with flexibility in imposition of sanctions
- recognition of need to 'escape' and provision of 'escape routes' for child
- a whole school approach involving all staff in contact with the child and a programme of active peer support ('buddy' systems, 'circles of friends')
- a programme to develop communication regardless of language level and resources to liaise with speech and language therapists to develop a context-based communication programme across the curriculum
- resources to liaise with occupational therapists or physiotherapists as appropriate for advice on the physical management of the learning environment and (where necessary) to provide programmes of posture control and physical development
- commitment to close home/school liaison with regular communication to ensure sharing of information, transfer of skills and consistency of programmes
- structuring of the environment and learning task to enable independent and group learning, using visual forms of instructions in preference to verbal instructions, as needed
- a programme to develop social and emotional understanding, utilising reflection , 'philosophy for children programmes and social stories and cartoons
- arrangements for asocial learning (e.g. computer assisted learning) to enable access to academic achievement without waiting for the development of the social skills necessary for group learning and social mediation
- specific teaching to control impulses and self-manage behaviour and an approach to difficult behaviour that concentrates on teaching more appropriate behaviour to serve the same function
- emphasis on building on strengths rather than teaching to deficits
- behaviour management systems that do not rely on physical manipulation or restraint.

Recommendation

1 All schools should have whole school ASD awareness training as part of regular supported INSET provision at least once every three years.

2 All specialist provision should have staff with a recognised qualification in autistic spectrum disorders or social and communication disorders (not just short term attendance at courses).

3 All schools should have access to specialist ASD staff (educational psychologist, advisory teachers, speech and language therapists and occupational therapists, as needed) and should be resourced for appropriate liaison with such staff.

4 Specialist schools should have mandatory arrangements for managed integration opportunities with mainstream pupils and all staff in mainstream schools should be resourced to gain from local specialist provision to develop skills and understanding and establish partnerships for shared expertise across settings, especially in relation to shared placement arrangements, integration and inclusion opportunities.

Statements (England and Wales) and Records (Scotland) of special educational needs

A diagnosis of ASD is important in directing a more accurate interpretation of the behaviour of the child and in opening up avenues of appropriate support and education. However, each child remains an individual and careful assessment of needs and strengths (including interests and learning style) is needed to inform individual educational plans. That much is generally accepted and reinforced by this report.

The question remains whether this assessment of needs should be formally identified and legally protected in a statement or record of needs. Paradoxically, this protection is most needed where it is least likely to occur. Thus, in a situation where local professionals are well aware of the needs arising from autistic conditions and services are well adapted to meet this range of needs, the child is most likely to have needs met without a statement or record. It is only where the needs of the child are not recognised by local professionals and services are unable or unwilling to adapt to those needs, that a legal protection may be needed to ensure the child and family gain access to what is required.

Yet even a legal statement or record of 'entitlement' cannot in reality always ensure the suitability of local services, change entrenched attitudes or inform and qualify professionals. In the long term, therefore, this report looks forward to a more inclusive system where a full range of local services are 'autism friendly' and there is minimal need for such legal protection. In the short and even medium term, however, some legally enforceable record or statement of a child's needs may well be needed and useful in alerting uninformed professionals of the nature of those needs if the needs are not being appropriately met at School Action or School Action Plus under the *SEN Code of Practice.*

The NIASA working group does not support the policy of limiting statements or records to a group arbitrarily defined in terms of academic ability as this is likely to discriminate against children with Asperger's syndrome or ASD without learning difficulties. It is also unacceptable to delay appropriate placement pending the production of a statement or record of needs. Just as appropriate provision and support should not wait for a formal diagnosis, nor should it wait for a formal description of needs. Placement or support may alter as needs are assessed and defined, but the process of identifying needs should occur as part of the educational process, not as an entry requirement.

Inclusion versus specialist educational provision

Knowing a child has an autistic spectrum disorder can never give the total picture and does not, of itself, determine the child's placement. There will always be a range of issues to consider when deciding on the best placement for a particular child and Jordan and Powell (1995) explore some of these in their advice to parents on choosing a school. There has been some research evidence that children with autistic spectrum disorders benefit from contact with normally developing peers and that this contact also benefits their classmates (Strain and Hoyson, 2000).

However, success is only documented in relation to well supported situations, where professionals are trained and mere placement (even with 1 to 1 support of an untrained teaching assistant) does not guarantee true inclusion or the meeting of needs (Jordan and Powell, 1994). There are some good examples of making non-specialist schools of all kinds autism-friendly and there are many initiatives for training support assistants, but the situation is very variable. It is important that local professionals (especially educational psychologists and LEA officers) understand the school and child variables that need to be considered in making a decision on placement. They must also be in a position to inform and support parents in making an informed choice.

There is no guarantee that labelling a provision as 'autism-specific' necessarily makes it so or that a local mainstream or general special needs school might not have as much expertise and understanding of ASD (or at least have sufficient, with other significant advantages). Jordan et al (2001) provide a rough guide for professionals on the different factors that might partly determine the degree of specialism versus inclusion best suited to the child at any one time. What is important is that decisions are not irrevocable and there should be greater flexibility in arrangements between specialist and other schools (whether or not either is independent or maintained) that facilitate (rather than just allow) a range of opportunities for integrated experiences and sharing of staff expertise across settings. The guiding principle of 'the least restrictive environment' is a sound one, providing that meeting the individual's needs (including the basic right to freedom from persecution, stress and distress) is a paramount consideration.

'ASD-friendly school provision'

As with pre-school provision, there are no single approaches that have been demonstrated to be better than other approaches (Jordan, Jones, and Murray, 1998). Most of the evaluative research on interventions in autism have concentrated on the goal of reducing the child's autism and on gross measures of development such as IQ (although the latter is as likely to reflect changes in the child's compliance rather than real IQ change). However, children with ASD also have the same rights and entitlements as other children to a broad and relevant curriculum experience to meet their needs and help them develop their potential. A good school for a child with autism, then, should enable the child to gain access to their entitlement and also enable the child to manage and live with their own autistic 'symptoms' to prevent emotional distress and behavioural disturbance. For the young child, or those with additional learning difficulties, the provision will need to be specially adapted to meet the child's needs.

As the child develops, however, it is the role of education to help the child develop his/her own strategies to manage their ASD and to learn to cope with a world which will not have such specialist adaptations. The art of teaching is to take the child along this route by steps that present challenges just sufficient to facilitate development and learning but not so great that the child is discouraged and frustrated. Some children may never reach a state of full independence, and most, no matter how great their academic skills and achievements, remain vulnerable and in need of some support throughout life. However, to paraphrase a young woman with autism – (Ros Blackburn, personal communication) it is important to have high expectations, as long as they are backed up with appropriate levels of support.

There are no curriculum subjects that of themselves are unsuitable for children with ASD, although there are aspects of many subjects where specific difficulties may arise. For example, teaching reading should not await a child's ability to relate a story or sequence pictures but should utilise many children with ASD capacity to be hyperlexic to build understanding of language, story structure and even aid speech development. Team games may be particularly problematic but should not automatically be ignored. It may be worth teaching the child systematically on a one to one basis to a level that allows participation so that the child eventually learns through practice, rather than becoming increasingly disabled in this activity through non participation. Children with ASD can be helped to participate in group activities by specific teaching of group cues and by managing the physical environment (i.e. allowing clearly marked personal space, placing the child so that no-one passes behind them) and introducing it by a process of gradual desensitisation.

Rita Jordan and Ann Le Couteur, Core Group Members

Special medical interventions – (see 4.3.2.3)

It is important to distinguish treatments for ASD from treatments aimed at the many associated co-morbid disorders. The latter include disorders that can amplify the ASD, such as epilepsy and depression, as well as numerous symptoms (as varied as sleep disturbance, obsessions and compulsions, attentional disturbance, bowel problems and aggression). However, the distinction is arbitrary and it is a matter of judgement, for example, at which point repetitive self-stimulation becomes self-injury. These symptoms can reflect a variety of problems ranging from communication problems through to physical discomfort and emotional malaise. While a treatment may have the intended, direct effect on the individual, the programme is also likely to affect the person's environment, their pattern of living and their relationships with other people, any of which may have a much more profound effect on their symptomatology.

There have been a large number of reports suggesting one treatment or another to be very effective only for further and more rigorous studies to have shown the effectiveness of a placebo to be as great - examples are the use of fenfluramine (du-Verglas, Banks, and Guyer, 1988) and secretin (Chez et al, 2000). These forays have taught us the hazards of evaluating a treatment. They have confirmed the extent to which ASD symptomatology changes over time. Not only does it vary from day to day but, as a developmental disorder, it alters with age; change occurring unevenly in a series of spurts, particularly in early childhood, early adolescence and as the person moves into adulthood. A third factor is the ability of an individual to adapt to change, whether shown by the loss of effectiveness of a reward programme or tolerance to a drug.

Some treatments hold some popular favour, such as naltrexone (Campbell, 1996) or an exclusion diet (Knivsberg et al, 1998). At present the level of evidence is such that it is not possible for the NIASA working group to make any definite recommendations either for or against specific therapies. Therefore, should a family determine to try an exclusion diet, this should proceed with appropriate medical and dietician/nutritional support.

ASD is a heterogeneous disorder and it is likely that should a treatment be effective, it would work only for a subset of people and then only for some of their symptoms. Consequently, it is to be expected that the profile of response (including both adverse and desired effects) for a given treatment will vary from person to person: every programme of treatment becoming a therapeutic trial for that individual.

Haloperidol has been the most thoroughly investigated of the neuroleptics and it has been shown to be effective in improving both the core and the associated symptoms of autism. Currently, however, haloperidol is no longer recommended as it has also been shown to be very likely to produce significant adverse effects. This now should seriously restrict its use (Campbell, 1999). Recent reports of newer, atypical neuroleptics, for example risperidone, appear encouraging. Serotoninergic drugs, such as fluoxetine, are also being used to treat symptoms such as anxiety. Low dose melatonin has also been used with individuals with significant sleep difficulties.

It usually takes a long time and widespread usage to establish the relative safety and benefits of a drug, particularly in childhood where its effect on maturation must be taken into account. Access to expert advice in paediatric psychopharmacology should be available to the local multi-disciplinary multi-agency team. Unfortunately, at present this is an unusual and specialist area for which the evidential base is limited. There are relatively few psychiatrists or paediatricians with experience in this field.

Practice point

In conclusion there is a place for the use of medication in the management of co-morbidity whether it is epilepsy, depression, behavioural or sleep disturbance and there are a number of reviews of this field (Gringras, 2000; Santosh, 1999).

Tom Berney and Ann Le Couteur, Core Group Members

v.   Professional groups: summary of existing 'minimum standards' for ASD training (see 4.6.3)

It was recognised by the NIASA Working Group that:
- The existing and planned roles of professional groups may vary in different local population units and regions across the United Kingdom.
- It is the expert skills and clinical judgement of the individuals within the GDA and MAA teams that are important, not necessarily their professional background.
- Core Group members were asked to provide a brief summary of minimum standards for ASD training for their professional group.
- This section is not exhaustive. For example Community and Inpatient Child and Adolescent Mental Health services and other Community Children's services consist of multi-disciplinary teams that can include clinical nurse specialists, learning disabilities nurses, child psychotherapists, and other therapy specialists. These professional groups were not separately represented on the Core Working Group but the Core Working Group acknowledges the importance of the three levels of specific ASD training for all professionals working directly with children and young people. These three levels of specific ASD training are:
  1   Training in increasing awareness of ASD is needed for all community based staff.
  2   Specific skills in the diagnostic assessment of ASD and related disorders is required for all professionals involved in Stage 2 Multi-Agency Diagnostic Assessment.
  3   Specific skills and enhanced understanding for all professionals involved in the delivery of intervention, education and support services for children with suspected ASD and their families.

Recommendations

The NIASA working group recommend that within a local population area ongoing joint multi-disciplinary/multi-agency training with parents/carers should be encouraged.

Reviews are undertaken by Core Group members unless otherwise stated.

General practitioner training

All undergraduate medical training must include autism spectrum disorders awareness, assessment and diagnosis. Training in the developmental needs of children and autism spectrum disorders experience should be included in the core child health curriculum during GP vocational training. Experience in the use of Parent Evaluation of Developmental Status (PEDS) and an awareness of the principles behind the Checklist for Autism in Toddlers (CHAT) should be considered. At postgraduate level teaching in child health as part of the postgraduate training programme should regularly include autism spectrum disorders. Training materials such as awareness raising videotapes and other training aides can also be included in continuing professional development (CPD) initiatives. Child health surveillance courses should include aspects of social communication development including joint attention and early play skills to update and enhance ASD awareness. There is also the need to consider co-morbidity in the field of developmental disorders. General practitioners who provide child health surveillance (CHS) services must attend a CHS course or show appropriate experience (such as the Diploma in Child Health). They should attend regular refresher courses, although this obligation is rarely enforced.

The ASD co-ordinating group, in collaboration with the Primary Care Trust (PCT) and GP tutors should encourage GPs in this obligation. The PCT will also have to ensure that those GPs not providing child health surveillance are sufficiently aware of ASD and the referral pathway.

Jamie Nicholls. Core Group Member

Health visitors and all community nursing staff working with children
For both these groups professional training in normal child development should include training to observe behaviours such as aspects of early social communication, joint attention and early interactive play skills. Graduate training should enhance these observational skills with further specific training in the use of particular behavioural assessment checklists such as the CHAT and PEDS. ASD awareness materials including the use of videotapes can also enhance training opportunities and the dissemination of knowledge.

Jenny Hugman, Core Group Member

Local education funded staff (working directly with children) including pre-school support staff, early educators, SENCOs, teachers, and classroom support staff
All staff should receive ASD awareness training. However, awareness training is not enough for those working specifically with children with an ASD. There is a need to accredit practical experience as part of a modularised training programme. The ability to make detailed informed observations about aspects of a child's behaviour and functioning is essential to enable education staff to consider each child's unique mixture of skills and deficits. Acknowledgement of the types of social communication skills children need to access learning should be included in core professional training. There are increasing LEA and Higher Institutions (HI) initiatives for Level 1 training of early educators, teachers and support staff.

The Teacher Training Agency standards – the *National Special Educational Needs Specialist Standards* (1999) – describe the 'extension standards' necessary to work within pupils on the autistic spectrum.

Training enhances the knowledge about specific disorders including autistic spectrum disorders. A number of training courses and programmes provide information about successful educational intervention strategies and approaches for teaching children with autistic spectrum disorders. Details of accredited programmes in ASD available at UK HE institutes are available from the NAS and the *Good Autism Practice Journal*. These programmes may be accessed by teachers, teaching support assistants and school based care workers as well as other local authority and health care and CAMHS staff, as appropriate for their CPD training needs and qualifications. Many LEAs also provide training programmes for staff, some of which are accredited through HE institutes.

Rita Jordan, Core Group Member

Speech and language therapists (SLTs)

Undergraduate training must include awareness of the early diagnostic pointers in relation to social communication, in order to differentiate between ASD and developmental language delay and disorder. Early diagnosis and intervention should be highlighted and students should be given opportunities to support their academic training with placements in a variety of settings including clinics and schools. SLTs are often among the first professionals to encounter young children with ASD because it is their difficulties with language and communication that alert parents to the fact that something may be wrong. It is therefore essential that SLTs working in the community have specific training skills for appropriate assessments and management of children with ASD.

At post graduate level SLTs must access accredited training courses if they want to be considered for specialist autistic spectrum disorders posts. Such courses need to be developed and expanded. Generalist SLTs should make use of the Regional Advisory Network which is provided by specialist SLTs who offer practical information and guidance over a wide range of topics in the field of autism. SLTs working in this field should be affiliated to an ASD special interest group.

It is also recommended that a further level of expertise should be acknowledged by the establishment of Consultant posts within the speech and language therapy profession. These will be for individuals with known expertise in the field of ASD which may include clinical practice, research, writing, teaching and training.

Maureen Aarons and Tessa Gittens, Core Group Members

Chartered clinical psychologists

In the UK all chartered clinical psychologists must have completed a training course accredited by the British Psychological Society. In addition, in order to work effectively with children with autism and their families, clinical psychologists should have:

- experience of working (under supervision) with children with a range of different disorders. This is necessary in order to experience the breadth of strategies that can be employed with children with very different disorders/developmental levels. Experience of other disorders is also important for developing better awareness of the very specific problems associated with autism
- undergone formal training *and supervision* in the administration, scoring and interpretation of standardised instruments designed to assess basic cognitive, language, play and self help skills. (See lists)
- experience of different methods for conducting observational assessments of children in home and school settings
- practical training in the use of behavioural approaches to intervention
- training in and experience of family based approaches
- familiarity with formal diagnostic criteria for childhood disorders generally and Autism Spectrum Disorders in particular
- training in the use of basic screening instruments (e.g. CHAT; ASQ)
- opportunities to observe and take part in multi-disciplinary diagnostic and assessment sessions

In addition, for psychologists working in specialised settings for children with developmental disorders, formal training in diagnostic and assessment techniques should be provided (e.g. ADOS and ADI-R training).

Pat Howlin, Core Group Member

Educational psychologists

- All educational psychologists (EPs) in England are trained and experienced teachers and will therefore have learnt how to make detailed informal observations of a child's behaviour and functioning in order to create a profile of a child's strengths and difficulties. Basic ASD awareness raising should also have been covered in initial teacher training but if it is not, it should be covered in all postgraduate Educational Psychology professional training courses. EP training should include a working knowledge of the 'alerting signals' for ASD and specific methods of observation, assessment and intervention to meet the needs of children with an ASD.
- Practising EPs need to ensure they are kept abreast of current thinking and research either by attending continuing professional development (CPD) courses on ASD or through in-house training delivered by specialist colleagues.
- EPs wishing to specialise in ASD should consider further modular courses in ASD.

They should know how to:
- identify the main characteristics of ASD and understand the factors contributing to varied expression in individuals
- assess the value of a range of diagnostic tools and be able to present information to contribute to multi-disciplinary diagnosis and assessment
- understand the barriers to learning and teaching in ASD and have strategies for working with schools and pre-school services in overcoming these
- understand the ontology of behavioural disturbance in ASD and be able to support schools and families in analysing behaviour and developing plans to prevent and manage challenging behaviour
- recognise stress-related behaviours in individuals with ASD and help schools, families and individuals implement strategies to reduce that stress
- understand the effects of ASD on all family members and have ways of helping families deal with and reduce their own stress
- work collaboratively with professionals across the health/social services interface with schools and families in meeting the needs of children with ASD
- evaluate interventions on an authority-wide basis and train staff and parents to make evaluations of their own practice.

Annette English, Core Group Member; Glenys Jones, University of Birmingham, and Jane Leadbetter, West Midlands SEN Regional Partnership

Social workers

Social workers working within child development centres, area offices, CAMHS or children's disability services should have core training in autism spectrum disorders as part of their career development. No social worker should be allocated to a child with an ASD without having undergone specific autism training and each district should have at least one member of staff for whom autism is a specific interest. Ongoing training in autism spectrum disorders should be an integral part of performance planning.

Christine Lenehan, Council for Disabled Children

Paediatricians and child health doctors

Undergraduates

The curriculum should include specific teaching about autism spectrum disorders, including aetiology as currently understood, diagnostic criteria, functional impact and co-morbidities.

All undergraduates should develop sufficient understanding of ASD that they recognise indicators of undiagnosed ASD, know where to refer for detailed assessment and are sympathetic to the functional challenges which the condition might present.

Knowledge and competence should be assessed as part of the assessment and examination process for medical students.

Paediatric trainees (and therefore consultant paediatricians of all specialties)
All trainees intending to pursue a career in Paediatrics should develop the competence to recognise children with potential ASD and to know how to achieve timely detailed assessment towards appropriate management. ASD is an important part of disability training and developmental paediatrics.

All trainees should develop a sufficient knowledge base about ASD to understand and be sympathetic to the functional consequences and to give basic advice and make appropriate on-referrals.

These competencies should be assessed as part of the Membership of the Royal College of Paediatrics and Child Health (MRCPCH) examination.

Consultants with special responsibility for paediatric neurodisability
The education and training subgroup of the RCPCH Standing Committee on Disability has produced a training pack which defines the competencies expected by the time of Consultant Certificate Specialist Training (CCST) for a paediatrician applying for a consultant post which requires special responsibility for paediatric neurodisability.

It is expected that these clinicians will recognise and be able to contribute to the multi-disciplinary/multi-agency assessments that leads to a possible diagnosis of ASD and a needs based family care plan (FCP), and know how and where to refer those children who present special diagnostic challenges. Competencies will be assessed using tools defined in the training pack.

Each district should have one disability specialist who has the competences for diagnosis of autism trained in using the specially developed frameworks for interview and observation. Such a person would have the competences for diagnosis and management of ASD and co-morbid disorders across their range of learning difficulties, be experienced in assessments, investigations and treatment options.
Gillian Baird, Core Group Member, Karen Whiting, Sunderland Royal Hospital and
Dianne Smyth, St Mary's Hospital

Child and adolescent mental health team members and other staff including clinical nurse specialist and inpatient unit staff, nursery staff, learning disability nurses, psychotherapists and other therapists will require ASD specific training (see comments as part of introductory section in (v) Professional groups – training on p96).

Psychiatrists
Child and adolescent psychiatry and child and adolescent learning disability psychiatry

Level 1 – Basic experience – the knowledge/skills required at MRCPsych level

Level 2 – Basic competence (the level that might be expected from any psychiatrist on appointment as a consultant). The psychiatrist as a member of an MAA team should be:

1 Able to contribute to the diagnosis or exclude the diagnosis of ASD in straightforward cases using standard diagnostic criteria.

2 Also able to recognise and/or diagnose those conditions that are often co-morbid or part of the differential diagnosis (learning disability, ADHD, Tourette syndrome, epilepsy, dyspraxia, mental illness).

3 Able to contribute to the development of a multi-agency intervention plan that includes psychological, educational and social contributions.

4 Know the indications, contraindications and limitations of the use of medication and other interventions. Recommending medication if necessary for co-morbid psychiatric conditions.

5 Able to work psychotherapeutically with the family and to help them to understand and come to terms with their child's disability.

6 Have an involvement with local support groups.

Level 3 – Specialist competence (the level that might be aimed for within a few years of consultant appointment and those with special responsibility for ASD. The psychiatrists should be:

1 Able to carry out a very full and comprehensive assessment of an individual with ASD (usually as a member of a team) including the more borderline and complex presentations. Training and/or experience of a standardised approach to taking a developmental history and observational assessment (e.g. ADI-R/ADOS, DISCO). A similar level of competence in the diagnosis of those conditions that are often co-morbid or part of the differential diagnosis.

2 Have experience and skills in initiating and leading the use of medication, psychotherapeutic and other interventions in the management of ASD as part of a multi-disciplinary intervention strategy.

3 Show experience and skills in working psychotherapeutically with those families who have found it very difficult to understand or come to terms with their child's disability.

4 Liaise with and consult providers of services for people with autism spectrum disorders.

5 Be involved in early intervention programmes, parent support groups and other activities supporting and informing families.

6 Have knowledge and ability to advise the Courts concerning the nature of a child's condition, its relevance to behaviour and the best ways of treating/managing the condition and fostering the child's development.

7 Able to play a lead role in the development of services – in conjunction with representatives of all relevant professional groups with ASD expertise.

8 Contribute to teaching and research on this topic and in related areas.

9 Have an awareness of other agencies providing ASD services.

Tom Berney and Ann Le Couteur, Core Group Members

vi. Regional and national ASD academic and training networks (June 2002)

Regional and national ASD network

1 Historically there have been very few clinical academic sites in the UK providing clinical and multi-agency training in the diagnosis of ASD. The existing sites provide training in the use of particular semi-structured instruments (namely the DISCO; ADI-R and ADOS); each requires specific training to administer the instrument reliably. The training courses have significant waiting lists (up to 2 years) and provide training for some research and some clinical staff. There has been no national training strategy to support local clinical local area developments.

2 For educational training and interventions, the Special Educational Needs Training Consortium in conjunction with the Autism Monitoring Group (a consortium of Higher Education educational trainers in ASD) has established standards of training and practice, which have been incorporated into the DfES and Teacher Training Agency approved standards for Specialist Training. The Confederation of Service Providers for People with Autism (COSPPA) has developed an induction pack for minimum standards for staff working with individuals with ASD.

3 The Autism Working Group of the DfES and DoH has issued *Good Practice Guidance* for ASD in the form of:

01 Guidance on autistic spectrum disorders and
02 Pointers to good practice.

These documents, are intended to give practical help to those 'who make provision for children with ASD'. An expanded version is available on-line at www.dfes.gov.uk/sen with examples of good practice from around the UK and from wide consultation.

4 A number of academic and independent institutions provide ASD specific training for parents/carers and professionals in different parts of the UK.

5 Much of the existing successful training in the UK has been developed in non clinical training institutes with a particular emphasis on learning and educational interventions. Distance learning courses provide ASD training for a range of professionals (including clinical and non clinical individuals) working with children with ASD. Call the NAS Information Centre 020 7903 3599 (open 10.00am-2.00pm weekdays) for details of appropriate training courses and programmes, or consult *Good Autism Practice Journal* (contact Publications Secretary, Autism West Midlands, 18 Highfield Road, Birmingham B15 3DU).

6 There is a need to develop a national training strategy and agree appropriate training courses and programmes for the different groups of professionals who need training in ASD awareness, diagnosis and appropriate interventions. There are significant resource and training implications that arise directly as a consequence of the recommendations outlined in this report.

7 The UK training capacity will need to expand to include the development of some new training sites, to fund the infrastructure support necessary to develop training programmes, to coordinate the training and to monitor the quality of the training initiatives.

8 Funding will be required to meet this considerable training agenda. Consideration should be given to joint collaborative funding initiatives involving the statutory authorities and voluntary charitable institutions and organisations.

9 The dangers of failure to ensure high quality for early identification, assessment, diagnosis and intervention, education and support services for children with ASD and their families is both the inevitable distress of unmet need and the inability for affected individuals to achieve their full potential.

One suggested model of UK training

- A **national network** of training centres could provide a co-ordinated response to the growing UK demand for high quality multi-agency training in early identification, accurate case ascertainment and diagnosis in ASD in close collaboration with existing education and training organisations and initiatives.

- The UK clinical and non clinical training needs and responsibilities should be overseen by a **UK ASD training committee**, with representation from the regional academic clinical centres, existing ASD training institutes, local area ASD co-ordinating groups, and relevant statutory and independent agencies (health, education, social services, voluntary parent and young people organisations).

- Such a training committee should audit current UK ASD training and develop a **UK wide training strategy** to meet the current clinical and non-clinical training needs.

- The resulting training strategy should develop a **network of regional training partnerships** involving existing academic regional clinical centres engaged in ASD collaborative research and training initiatives (using the currently recognised diagnostic assessment tools employed in most multi site research collaborations).

- The next step should be to increase collaboration and cooperation between smaller specialist clinical sites with existing clinical and non-clinical training centres. Some of these specialist clinical sites may be providing diagnostic and intervention services but not have the capacity to provide ASD specific training. Collaboration between existing academic clinical training sites, other clinical and non clinical training sites using innovative training methods for multi-agency training with ASD families (such as distance education, and/or web training) would also increase training capacity.

- A network of mobile training teams supervised by each regional training partnership could provide individualised programmes of multi-agency and multi-disciplinary training appropriate for the differing training needs of local area services.

- Once a national training strategy has been established, the success of local training initiatives should be audited for each regional network and new initiatives evaluated against national examples of best practice.

- Further, as academic progress is made in ASD research, new diagnostic assessment instruments will be required for both clinical and research work. The UK ASD Training committee should co-ordinate both the development of new diagnostic and outcome measures and the dissemination of best practice throughout the UK.

- The UK ASD training committee should oversee training programmes for:

Level 1
Joint local multi-disciplinary and multi-agency programmes of ASD awareness training on a continuous basis for all professionals working with children in the community and for parents/carers.

Level 2

(a) ASD specific training for all those providing assessment and diagnosis of ASD.

(b) Training for all staff delivering both specific ASD interventions and other interventions for children with ASD (not limited to a single intervention approach).

Level 3

Training in use of ASD specific research diagnostic tools and specific research assessments to evaluate outcome and the changing characteristics of this group of children with life long developmental disorders.

Ann Le Couteur, Core Group Chair

vii.   Research and evaluation

Much progress has been made over the last forty or so years in the recognition and understanding of autism (Rutter, 2001). In more recent years there has been a greater awareness of the broader spectrum of autism disorders and an increasing interest in early detection and access to early interventions for these disorders.

It is now generally recognised that autism is an organic, neurodevelopmental disorder and that genetic factors play an important role in the aetiology of both autism and the broader autism spectrum. Progress has been made in our understanding of some of the underlying neuropsychological deficits, the biological underpinnings and the genetic findings. A number of recent reviews have focused on particular aspects of research in ASD (MRC, 2001; New York State Department of Health, 1999; Lord et al, 2001). All these reviews have highlighted the importance of high quality research and emphasise the need to build on research strengths; to identify opportunities for multidisciplinary collaborative research; to develop methodologies that answer professionals' and carers' concerns and build on existing knowledge.

The *MRC Review of Autism Research* 2001 was a joint professional/scientific and lay group collaboration undertaken by the Medical Research Council at the request of the UK Department of Health, to review research on the causes and epidemiology of autism. The report concluded with a proposed set of strategic themes to take forward research on ASD. The *New York State Review* 1999 provided a systematic review of interventions currently in use in the United States and concluded that the standard of experimental research was poor and that further research was required to answer specific questions relevant to the assessment and management of individuals with suspected ASD. In *Educating Children with Autism*, Lord et al (2001) focused on educational interventions but again concluded that there was a lack of rigorous scientific evaluation studies.

High quality research is essential to the development of evidence based practice that can in turn be incorporated in family care plans. There is evidence of the effectiveness of a range of intervention approaches (in particular behavioural and educational approaches). However, many unanswered questions remain.

The *National Autism Plan for Children* and the *MRC Review* have identified a number of UK strengths, which offer opportunities to enhance research capacity and research requirements. There is a need to develop across the UK:

(i) A network of research centres that facilitate lay and service provider participation within researcher-funder partnerships. These partnerships should then develop agreed research priorities. Increased lay participation will inform research priorities and reduce the apparent gulf between scientific research and the unanswered questions that are often the subject of anxiety and speculation amongst the general public.

(ii) A national strategy that strengthens the interface between service delivery and the research groups undertaking high quality ASD research. This would have a number of benefits including the dissemination of research findings to enable the promotion of evidence based practice, the building of closer relationships between relevant research outcomes and the intended beneficiaries; enhance relevant intervention evaluation and effectiveness studies and promote training in appropriately informed assessment and intervention techniques.

Research priorities

I   **Identification of ASD**
Taking into account the complex ethical considerations, there is still a need for further research on early screening for ASD. This should involve the refinement of potential screening tools and investigation of the impact of screening on families and service providers.

II   **What is autism/ASD?**
The definition of ASD is fundamental to all research questions. The development of specific assessment tools for core autism and the broader spectrum of ASD has been a UK strength. In the light of new findings on the prevalence of ASD and the broadening of the diagnostic spectrum, there is a need to re-evaluate and revise existing diagnostic tools and develop new reliable and valid instruments for diagnostic assessment and outcome evaluation studies. Once such diagnostic assessment tools have been developed and appropriately tested there will be an ongoing need to train sufficient numbers of individuals in the reliable use of these tools to meet the manpower requirements for both high quality research and appropriate levels of service delivery. What are the assessment tools required to make a reliable and accurate diagnosis of individuals with differing levels of ability at different stages of development across the life-span?

Further studies are needed to investigate and describe specific phenotypic characteristics of ASD, to ascertain the longer term consequences of particular behavioural characteristics, the diagnostic validity of potential sub-groups and the overlap with other developmental disorders. ASD research registers and specifically targeted cohort studies would allow the formal testing of causal hypotheses and the investigation of possible genetic and environmental influences. Further research is also needed to investigate the impact of diagnosis/diagnoses on carers and the longitudinal significance of early pre-school diagnosis when compared with those individuals who receive a diagnosis at a later age. Population based studies within an epidemiological framework enable the testing of the prevalence of specific symptoms, case definition, natural history, co-morbidity and outcome studies.

III   **Investigations of related developmental skills and needs**
Alongside the diagnosis of ASD, there is the need for specific assessment tools to investigate related skills and needs (e.g. cognition, communication and language, mental health and behaviour, etc.). There is no database to govern decisions about which tests are most suitable for which children of a particular age or level of development. Research is needed to identify the most valid and reliable tests for use with children with ASD of different ages/ability levels, both for the assessment of

general and specific skills. There is also a need for research into the relationship between specific tests and the stability of scores from different tests over time.

IV   **How common is ASD?**

A number of recent epidemiological studies have now confirmed that autism spectrum disorders are among the most common developmental disorders of childhood. The UK has strengths in its population-based studies, especially in the use of regional databases. Such databases, when maintained over time, enable longitudinal studies to track any changes in prevalence. Population based studies within an epidemiological framework enable the testing of the natural history of symptoms of ASD, co-morbidity and outcome studies.

Specifically targeted cohort studies would allow the formal testing of causal hypotheses and the investigation of possible genetic and environmental influences. New epidemiological studies that incorporate genetic data will allow for the fairly rapid further investigation of gene-environment interaction. Such studies will pose challenges not least the need for national/international scientific collaboration.

V   **What are the causes of ASD and what investigations should be undertaken?**

In common with most medical conditions, ASD is likely to be a multi-factorial condition or group of conditions. Much scientific progress has been made investigating the genetic susceptibility. The current consensus is that several genes may interact to create the susceptibility to ASD. Genetic studies may identify ASD sub-groups. Further genetically sensitive research designs will inform our understanding of the role of possible environmental risk factors. As yet there are few replicated findings and many unanswered questions in relation to possible physiological and physical abnormalities in individuals with ASD.

Co-morbid medical conditions, behaviour abnormalities and mental health disorders

These have increasingly been recognised in association with cases of ASD. The *MRC Review* (2001) has outlined potential research strategies to investigate these associations further. The population based study of the range of co-morbid disorders in ASD linked to the longitudinal study over time will identify populations at risk for co-morbid psychiatric disorder and the impact on outcome. The identification of predictive factors will inform appropriate levels of assessment and in turn evidence based clinical practice.

Medical investigations

The report of small scale studies on abnormalities of gut function, gut permeability and related abnormal findings such as plasma sulphate, needs to be repeated in large epidemiological based samples with appropriate controls. Is there an increased rate of bowel disorders in children with ASD? What investigations should be undertaken and how should this influence treatment strategies? These and related questions are frequently presented by individual families and their representatives.

The relevance and significance of epileptiform EEG abnormalities in children with ASD at varying developmental ages and at developmental levels also needs further investigation.

Genetic and family studies

Further hypothesis driven studies to investigate rates of disorder amongst relatives of those with ASD, language disorders, developmental co-ordination disorders and related developmental difficulties will inform understanding of the wider ASD phenotype and the development of appropriately targeted specific interventions.

Significant progress has been made in the development of several psychological theories that may help to explain the nature of specific symptoms in ASD. A full psychological understanding of ASD should inform both studies of the neurobiological basis and appropriate intervention approaches for ASD.

Underlying brain behaviour relationships

Further research is needed to explore the links between underlying neurobiological structure and the behavioural consequences of such abnormalities. The understanding of normal and abnormal development of psychological functions will in turn inform intervention strategies i.e. moving from theoretical underpinning to effective evidence based practice. It will also be essential to elucidate brain behaviour mechanisms from molecular genetic findings through to the study of physiological and neuropathological consequences of particular genetic constitutions. It is hoped that this in turn will lead to the development of new informed interventions. Inevitably as described by Rutter (2001) there is a long way from the identification of genes to therapy.

VI **What are the most effective interventions in ASD?**
There is no good evidence for the use of one particular intervention or therapy over another. The National Autism Plan for Children report provides a guide to current best practice. In determining the agenda for intervention research there should be a focus on approaches that are relevant and appropriate in the UK. The research agenda should not be driven by educational 'fashions/whims'; legal rulings or topics that are the focus of attention in other countries. Appropriate research strategies can take a variety of different forms from single case designs, multiple baseline case series, case-control studies or randomised controlled trials. In the initial stages of evaluating the potential value of any approach to intervention, single case or small group designs will be required.

However, no design other than a randomised controlled trial can avoid bias resulting from unmeasured confounding factors. It is necessary to develop a framework within which randomised trials can be successfully conducted across several sites/centres in order to develop sufficient power to determine whether any specific approach is superior to others. These studies must include access to educational interventions and all strategies that appear to offer something of potential value to parents.

Other intervention studies that need to be undertaken across research centres to ensure a sufficiently large cohort of affected children include:

(i) The investigation of potentially modifiable environmental risk factors.

(ii) The identification of which components of behavioural and educational intervention programmes are most effective.

(iii) Intervention research also needs to focus on the issue of which treatments work best for which particular children at which stages of development and within which family and social context. It is unrealistic to assume that any one approach will be appropriate for all children regardless of age, ability and family background. Are there individual characteristics that impact on outcome? These questions apply to general and specific interventions for both children, parents and other family members. It is also important to identify appropriate measurable outcome features. Although there has been successful focus on the importance of developing effective social communication skills in children with ASD and on the specific focus of helping parents foster communicative interactions in early development, there is very little information on the views of young people themselves through childhood, adolescence and into early adult life.

(iv) Appropriate strategies to evaluate interventions are needed. These should include medical intervention studies (including psychopharmacological medication), the use of dietary additives as well as the treatment of co-morbid disorders, especially mental health and behavioural disorders.

(v) Evaluation of service provision for families is also required, eg. respite care, behavioural support and joint funding between agencies for children with challenging behaviour who may need more specialist facilities.

VII   ASD training and evaluation

The *National Autism Plan for Children* has highlighted current UK training needs for carers and for professionals across disciplines. This applies both to clinical practice and the training of research teams in the use of appropriate diagnostic assessment tools and to all those staff supporting individuals with ASD and their families in a wide variety of intervention opportunities.

VIII   Audit timeframes and targets

The *National Autism Plan for Children* has identified achievable timeframe and service specification targets. These can be used to audit existing multi-agency services against the templates outlined in the report. Further, the recommendations of this report based on existing research findings and examples of best practice, provide a framework to inform the development of local practice, regional and national networks.

The core group strongly endorses the concluding comments of the MRC Review on Autism research. There is an urgent need to develop national strategies to nurture the research-service interface. This report provides a template for the co-ordination of a number of UK centres working in collaboration to provide professional training for the assessment and diagnosis of ASD for both researchers and clinicians. The funding and resource implications make it imperative that there is a national strategy to establish further partnerships of researchers, funders, service users and their representatives and direct service providers. Such partnerships will enhance scientific understanding, research capacity and the dissemination of new evidence based findings.

The National Service Framework for Children in collaboration with other national initiatives endorse the training and research recommendations outlined in this report.

Ann Le Couteur
Core Group Chair

Appendix B

In Appendix B details of evidence used to inform the recommendations are presented.

i. **Presentations on a series of key topics were made to the NIASA working group from a wide range of experts in the field of autistic spectrum disorders. Listed below are the titles of the presentations. Lists of speakers and further details are available on the NAS website www.nas.org.uk**

Presentation topics

- Identification: screening and surveillance for autistic spectrum disorders for pre-school and school age children – (9 May 2001)

- Investigations: investigations for children diagnosed with ASD – (5 July 2001)

- Assessment: diagnosis and assessment of ASD at 'district' level in the UK – (16 August 2001)

- Interventions: Evaluation of Early Educational Intervention, Continuity of Education and Care provision – (12 October 2001)

- Development of NIASA guidelines: Districts – (31 October 2001)

- Preliminary presentation on the guidelines and their implications (29 January 2002) to invited audience

ii. **NIASA survey results**

Survey of current practice in Child Health Services 2001
As part of a mapping exercise of existing services, the Working Group wrote to the 313 child development services (286 teams/centres) on the BACCH (British Association of Community Child Health) data base. The 286 child development teams or centres come from 127 different Health Authorities, Health Boards and Health Commissions in England, Scotland Wales and Northern Ireland. Since this survey was undertaken, District and Health Authorities have disappeared in the Health Service reorganisation.

Respondents (individuals, often but not exclusively doctors, are identified on the BACCH database) were asked whether their district had a screening program for ASD, if so which test was used; whether there was a written protocol for referral of suspected ASD; whether there was a multi-disciplinary assessment team for ASD separate from the general developmental assessment, and whether specific diagnostic instruments were used and if so, what they were. Respondents were also asked if CAMH services were an integral part of the child development service, if so, which professionals were involved; also if regular joint assessments were conducted and if so, for what age groups of children. Many indicated that their services were in active discussion about autism services.

Replies were received from 114/127 Health Authorities, Boards or Commissions, 240/286 teams/centres. (Some respondents described a service covering several districts.) Those who had written protocols sent them.

Results are expressed as a percentage of 240 replies.

1 9% had a primary (total population) screening program for autism, most using the CHAT.
2 40% of services had a multi-disciplinary assessment that was autism specific and separate from their usual CDS assessment (Stage 1).
3 31% had a written protocol for referral of suspected ASD from primary to secondary services and a further 5% had one in preparation. Many district services for ASD organised themselves on an age basis, e.g. concerns in a pre-school child were referred to the CDS/T and school age concerns to CAMHS.
4 14% used ADI or DISCO. The same numbers used ADI as DISCO.
5 38% (91) teams said that CAMHS were integral in the child development service. This was usually through a psychologist, employed by mental health but working in child development. (This does not necessarily represent the number of child development services who have a psychologist as some are employed directly by child health rather than through a mental health trust, however several respondents indicated that although there was establishment for psychology, there were frequently vacant posts and many comments were made about the absence of crucial personnel for comprehensive assessment especially a psychologist.) 6 services only (2.5%) had an educational psychologist working as part of the MD team. In 20% (48 teams) a psychiatrist was regularly involved in the child development service (in 3% a Learning Disability psychiatrist). 35 (14.6%) child health services held joint assessments with CAMHS for children/young people with suspected ASD. 3 services (1%) had a psychotherapist/parent counsellor or nurse therapist. 4 replies commented on the excellence of their liaison although there was no CAMH service incorporated in the child development service.

Gillian Baird, Core Group Member

iii. Background papers and literature review

Aarons, M., and Gittens, T. (1992). *The autistic continuum: an assessment and intervention schedule.*: Windsor: NFER-Nelson.

American Psychiatric Association. (1994). *Diagnostic and Statistical Manual for mental disorders.* (DSM-IV) 4th ed. Washington: APA.

American Psychological Association (1994). *Resolution on Facilitated Communication.* Washington DC: APA.

Anderson, S. R. and Romanczyk, R. G. (1999). Continuum-based behavioural models. *Journal for Persons with Severe Handicaps*, **24**, pp. 162–173.

Attwood, T. (1998). *Asperger's syndrome: a guide for parents and professionals.* London: Jessica Kingsley.

Autism Working Group. (2002) *Autistic spectrum disorders: good practice guidance.* 2 vols. London: Department for Education and Skills and Department of Health.

Bailey, A. (2002). Physical examination and medical investigations. In: Michael Rutter & Eric Taylor (eds.), *Child and adolescent psychiatry*, 4th ed., pp. 141-161. Oxford: Blackwell Science Publishing.

Bailey, A. et al (1995). Autism as a strongly genetic disorder: evidence from a British twin study. *Psychological Medicine*, **25**, pp. 63-77.

Bailey, A. et al. (1998). Autism: the phenotype in relatives. *Journal of Autism and Developmental Disorders*, **28**(5), pp. 369-392.

Bailey, D.B. et al (1998). Autistic behaviour in young boys with fragile X syndrome. *Journal of Autism and Developmental Disorders,* **28(6)**, pp. 499-508.

Baird, G., Charman, T., and Baron-Cohen, S. (2000). A screening instrument for autism at 18 months of age: a six-year follow-up study. *Journal of the American Academy of Child and Adolescent Psychiatry*, **39**, pp. 694-702.

Barnard, J., Prior, A. and Potter, D. (2000). *Inclusion and autism: is it working?* London: The National Autistic Society.

Baron-Cohen, S. et al (2000). Early identification of autism by the CHecklist for Autism in Toddlers (CHAT). *Journal of the Royal Society of Medicine*, **93**, pp. 521-525.

Baron-Cohen, S., Allen, J., and Gillberg, C. (1992). Can autism be detected at 18 months? The needle, the haystack, and the CHAT. *British Journal of Psychiatry*, **161**, pp. 839-843.

Barton, M., and Volkmar, F. (1998). How commonly are known medical conditions associated with autism? *Journal of Autism and Developmental Disorders*, **28**, pp. 273-278.

Bayley, N. (1993) *Bayley scales II.* London: Psychological Corporation.

Bebko, J.M., Perry, A., and Bryson, S. (1996). Multiple method validation study of facilitated communication: II Individual differences and subgroup results. *Journal of Autism and Developmental Disorders*, **26**, pp. 19-42.

Bernard, P. (2000). *Autistic spectrum disorders – an aide-memoire for interviewing parents/carers of young children.* Personal communication.

Bertrand, J. et. al. (2001). Prevalence of autism in a United States population: the Brick Township investigations. *Pediatrics*, **108**, pp.1155-1161.

Berument, S. K. et al (1999). Autism screening questionnaire: diagnostic validity. *British Journal of Psychiatry*, **175**, pp. 444-451.

Bishop, D.V.M. and Norbury-Frazier, C. (2002). Exploring the borderlands of autistic disorder and specific language impairment: a study using standardised diagnostic instruments. *Journal of Child Psychology and Psychiatry and Allied Disciplines*, **43** (7), pp. 917-929

Bolton, P. et al. (1998). Autism, affective and other psychiatric disorders: patterns of familial aggregation. *Psychological Medicine*, **28,** pp. 385-395.

Bolton, P., Macdonald, H., and Pickles, A.E.A. (1994). A case-control family history study of autism. *Journal of Child Psychology and Psychiatry and Allied Disciplines*, **35**, pp. 877-900.

Bowler, D. M., and Strom, E. (1998). Elicitation of first-order 'theory of mind' in children with autism. *Autism*, **2** (1), pp. 33-44.

Bristol, M. M. et al. (1985). Mothers and fathers of young developmentally disabled and non-disabled boys: adaptation and spousal support. *Developmental Psychotherapy*, **24**, pp. 441-451.

Bromley J. et al (2002). *Health and social care needs of families and/or carers supporting a child with autistic spectrum disorders*. www.lancs.ac.uk/depts/ihr/research/learning/projects/autism.htm

Campbell, M. (1996). Resolved: autistic children should have a trial of naltrexone: affirmative. *Journal of the American Academy of Child and Adolescent Psychiatry*, **35**, (2), pp. 246-247.

Campbell, M. et al. (1990). Stereotypes and tardive dyskinesia: abnormal movements in autistic children. *Psychopharmacology Bulletin*, **26**, pp.260-266.

Carr, E. G. et al. (1999). *Positive behaviour support for people with developmental disabilities*. Washington, D. C.: Mental Retardation Monograph Series.

Celiberti, D. A. and Harris, S. L. (1993). Behavioural intervention for siblings of children with autism: a focus on skills to enhance play. *Behaviour therapy*, **24**, pp. 573-599.

Chakrabarti, S., and Fombonne, E. (2001). Pervasive developmental disorders in pre-school children. *Journal of American Medical Association*, **285**, pp. 3093-3099.

Charman, T., and Baird, G. (2002). Practitioner review: diagnosis of autism spectrum disorder in 2- and 3-year-old children. *Journal of Child Psychology and Psychiatry and Allied Disciplines*, **43**, pp. 289-305.

Charman, T. and Howlin, P. (in press). Research into early intervention for children with autism and related disorders: methodological and design issues. Report on a workshop funded by the Wellcome Trust, Institute of Child Health, London, UK. *Autism*.

Chez, M. G., et al. (2000). Secretin and autism: a two-part clinical investigation. *Journal of Autism and Developmental Disorders*, **30**(2), pp. 87-94.

Christie, P. et al (1992). An interactive approach to language and communication for non-speaking children. In *Child and adolescent therapy: a handbook*. Milton Keynes: Open University Press.

Chugani, D. C. (2000). Autism. In: Ernst, M. and Rumsey, J. M. (eds.) *Functional neuroimaging in child psychiatry*. Cambridge: Cambridge University Press, pp. 171-188.

Cochrane, A., and Holland, W. (1969). Validation of screening procedures. *British Medical Bulletin*, **27**, pp. 3-8.

Cox, A., et al (1999). Autism spectrum disorders at 20 and 42 months of age: stability of clinical and ADI-R diagnosis. *Journal of Child Psychology and Psychiatry and Allied Disciplines*, **40**, pp. 719-732.

Cumine, V., Leach, J., and Stevenson, G. (1998). *Asperger syndrome: a practical guide for teachers*. London: David Fulton.

Cumine, V, Leach, J., and Stevenson, G. (2000). *Autism in the early years: a practical guide*. London: David Fulton.

Dawson, G., and Osterling, J. (1997). Early intervention in autism: effectiveness and common elements of current approaches. In: Guralnick, M. J. (ed.) *The effectiveness of early intervention*. Baltimore: Paul H. Brookes, pp. 307-326.

Dawson, G. and Watling, R. (2000). Interventions to facilitate auditory, visual and motor integration in autism: a review of the evidence. *Journal of Autism and Developmental Disorders*, **30**, pp. 415-421.

Department of Health (2001). *Valuing People*. London: Stationery Office.

Diggle, T., McConachie, H. and Randle, V. (2002). Parent mediated early intervention for young children with autism spectrum disorder. (Cochrane Review). *The Cochrane Library*, **1**.

DiLalla, D. L. and Rogers, S. (1994). Domains of the Childhood Autism Rating Scale: relevance for diagnosis and treatment. *Journal of Autism and Developmental Disorders*, **24** (2), pp. 115-128.

du Verglas, G., Banks, S. R., and Guyer, K. E. (1988). Clinical effects of fenfluramine on children with autism: a review of the research. *Journal of Autism and Developmental Disorders*, **18** (2), pp. 297-308.

Dunn, W. (1999) *The sensory profile*. London: Psychological Corporation.

Dunn, W. and Fisher A. (1983) Sensory registration, autism and tactile defensiveness. *Sensory Integration Special Interest Section Newsletter*, **6**(2) pp. 3-4.

Dunn-Geier, J., Ho, H.H., and Auersperg, E. et al (2000). Effects of secretin on children with autism: a randomized controlled trial. *Developmental Medicine and Child Neurology*, **42**, pp.796-802.

Dwand, B. M. and Carr, E. G. (1991). Functional communication training to reduce challenging behaviour. Maintenance and application in new settings. *Journal of Applied Behaviour Analysis*, **24**, pp. 251-254.

Elliott, C. (1996). *The British ability scales*. 2nd ed. Windsor: NFER-Nelson.

English, A. (2002). *Protocols for the identification, assessment and diagnosis of autistic spectrum disorders in the West Midlands*. West Midlands SEN Regional Partnership.

English, A., and Essex, J. (2001). *Report on autistic spectrum disorders: a comprehensive report into identification, training and provision focusing on the needs of children and young people with autistic spectrum disorder and their families within the West Midlands region*. Warwick: Warwickshire County Council for the West Midlands SEN Regional Partnership.

Ermer, J., and Dunn, W. (1998). The Sensory Profile: a discriminant analysis of children with and without disabilities. *American Journal of Occupational Therapy*, **52**, pp. 283-290.

Fatemi, S. H. et al. (1998). Fluoxetine in treatment of adolescent patients with autism: a longitudinal open trial. *Journal of Autism and Developmental Disorders*, **29**, pp. 303-307.

Filipek, P. A., et al (1999). The screening and diagnosis of autistic spectrum disorders. *Journal of Autism and Developmental Disorders*, **29**(6), pp. 439-484.

Filipek, P.A., et al (2000).Practice parameter: screening and diagnosis of autism. Report of the quality standards subcommittee of the American Academy of Neurology and the Child Neurology Society. *Neurology*, **55**(4), pp. 468-479.

Folstein, S. E., et al (1999). Predictors of cognitive test patterns in autism families. *Journal of Child Psychology and Psychiatry and Allied Disciplines*, **40**, pp.1117-1128.

Fombonne, E. (1999). Epidemiological surveys of autism: a review. *Psychological Medicine*, **29**, pp. 769-786.

Fombonne, E. (2001). Epidemiological investigations of autism and other pervasive developmental disorders. In: Lord, C. ed. *Educating children with autism*. Washington, DC: National Academy of Sciences Press.

Fombonne, E., et al (1997a). Autism and associated medical disorders in a large French epidemiological sample. *Journal of the American Academy of Child and Adolescent Psychiatry*, **36**, pp. 1561-1569.

Fombonne, E., et al (1997b). A family study of autism: cognitive patterns and levels in parents and siblings. *Journal of Child Psychology and Psychiatry and Allied Disciplines*, **38**, pp. 667-683.

Fombonne, E., et al (1999). Microcephaly and macrocephaly in autism. *Journal of Autism and Developmental Disorders*, **29**, pp.113-119.

Frith, U. (1991). *Autism and Asperger's Syndrome*. Cambridge: Cambridge University Press.

Ghaziuddin, M. and Greden, J. (1998). Depression in children with autism/pervasive developmental disorders: a case-control family history study. *Journal of Autism and Developmental Disorders*, **28**, pp. 111-115.

Gilchrist, A. et al (2001). Developed and current functioning in adolescents with Asperger syndrome: a comparative study. *Journal of Child Psychology and Psychiatry and Allied Disciplines*, **42**, pp. 227-240.

Gillberg, C. and Coleman, M. (1996) Autism and medical disorders: a review of the literature. *Developmental medicine and child neurology*, **38**, pp.191-202.

Gillberg, C. and Coleman, M. (2000) The biology of the autism syndrome. 3rd ed. London: MacKeith Press.

Gillberg, I.C., Gillberg, C. and Ahlsen, G. (1994) Autistic behaviour and attention deficits in tuberous sclerosis: a population-based study. *Developmental Medicine and Child Neurology*, **36**(1), pp. 50-6.

Glascoe, F. P., MacLean, W. E., and Stone, W. L. (1991). The importance of parents' concerns about their child's behavior. *Clinical Pediatrics*, **30**, pp. 8-11.

Green, J. et al. (2000). Social and psychiatric functioning in adolescents with Asperger's Syndrome compared with conduct disorder. *Journal of Autism and Developmental Disorders, 30*, pp. 279-293.

Griffiths, R. F. (1967). *Griffiths Mental Development Scales*. Henley on Thames: Association for Research in Infant and Child Development.

Gringras, P. (2000). Practical paediatric psychopharmacological prescribing in autism: the potential and the pitfalls. *Autism, 4*, pp. 229-247.

Hagerman, R.J., Jackson, A.W., Levistas, A et al (1986) An Analysis of Autism in Fifty Males with Fragile X Syndrome. *American Journal of Medical Genetics, 23*, pp. 359-74.

Hall, D., (1996), *Health for all children. The report of the Joint Working Party on Child Health Surveillance*. Oxford: Oxford University Press.

Handleman, J. S. and Harris, S. L. (2000). *Pre-school education programs for children with autism*. Austin TX: Pro-Ed Inc.

Harris, S. L. et al (1991). Changes in cognitive and language functioning in pre-school children with autism. *Journal of Autism and Developmental Disorders, 21*, pp. 281-290.

Harris, S. L. and Handleman, J. S. (2000). Age and IQ at intake as predictors of placement for young children with autism: a four-to-six year follow-up. *Journal of Autism and Developmental Disorders, 30*, pp. 137-142.

Hart, A., Geldard, H., and Geldard, P. (2000). *Inclusion – the parents view*. Spennymoor: County Durham Autistic Support Group. (PO Box 35,Spennymoor, Co. Durham, DL16 6GL)

Holland, T. (2000) Current issues surrounding the diagnosis, management and treatment of children and adults with Asperger's syndrome. Cambridge: University of Cambridge.

Howlin, P. (1998) Practitioner review: psychological and educational treatments for autism. *Journal of Child Psychology and Psychiatry and Allied Disciplines, 39*, pp. 307-322.

Howlin, P., and Asgharian, A. (1999). The diagnosis of autism and Asperger's syndrome: findings from a survey of 770 families. *Developmental Medicine and Child Neurology, 41*, pp. 834-839.

Howlin, P. and Charman, A. (2001). Presentation to NIASA Working Group.

Howlin, P., and Moore, A. (1997). Diagnosis in autism: A survey of over 1200 patients in the UK. *Autism*, 1, pp. 135-162.

Howlin, P. and Rutter, M. (1987). *Treatment of autistic children*. Chichester: John Wiley & Sons.

Hunt, A. and Shepherd, C. (1993). A Prevalence Study of Autism in Tuberous Sclerosis. *Journal of Autism and Developmental Disorders, 23*, pp. 323-339.

Hurth, J. et al. (1999) Areas of agreement about effective practices among programs serving young children with autism spectrum disorders. *Infants and Young Children, 12*, pp. 17-26.

Hutton, J. et al (in preparation). *Deterioration in autism – adult follow-up*.

Jordan, R. (2001). Presentation to NIASA Working Group.

Jordan, R., and Jones, G. (1999). *Meeting the needs of children with autistic spectrum disorders*. London: David Fulton.

Jordan, R., Jones, G., and Murray, D. (1998). *Educational interventions for children with autism: a literature review of recent and current research*. (Research Report 77) London: Department for Education and Employment.

Kaufman, A. S. and N. L. (1983). *Kaufman assessment battery for children*. Circle Pines, Minnesota: American Guidance Service.

Kerr, A. (2002). Annotation: Rett Syndrome: recent progress and implications for research and clinical practice. *Journal of Child Psychology and Psychiatry and Allied Disciplines, 43* (3), pp. 277-287.

Knivsberg, A., et al. (1998). Parents' observations after one year of dietary intervention for children with autistic syndromes. In: *Psychobiology of autism: current research and practice: a collection of papers from the conference held at Van Mildert College, University of Durham*. Sunderland: Autism Research Unit, pp. 13-24.

Koegel, R. L. and Koegel, L. K. (1995). *Teaching children with autism: strategies for imitating positive interactions and improving learning opportunities*. Baltimore: Brookes.

Koegel, L. K. (2000). Interventions to facilitate communication in autism. *Journal of Autism and Developmental Disorders,* **30**, pp. 383-392.

Lansing, M.and Schopler, E. (1978). Individualised education: a public school model. In M. Rutter and E. Schopler (eds) *Autism: a reappraisal of concepts and treatment.* New York: Plenum.

Le Couteur, A., Lord, C., and Rutter, M. (in press). *The Autism Diagnostic Interview – Revised (ADI-R).* Los Angeles, CA: Western Psychological Services.

Leekam, S., et al. (2002). The Diagnostic Interview for Social and Communication disorders: algorithms for ICD-10 childhood autism and Wing and Gould autistic spectrum disorder. *Journal of Child Psychiatry and Psychology and Allied Disciplines*, **43**, pp. 327-342.

Lewine, J. D. et al. (1999). Magnetoencephalographic patterns of epileptiform activity in children with regressive autism spectrum disorders. *Paediatrics*, **104**, pp. 405-418.

Lewis, K.E. et al. (1995). Chromosomal abnormalities in a psychiatric population. *American Journal of Medical Genetics*, **60**, pp. 53-4

Lewis, V. and Boucher, J. (1995). Generativity in the play of young people with autism. *Journal of Autism and Developmental Disorders*, **25**, pp. 105-121.

Lord, C. (2000). Achievements and future directions for intervention research in communication and autism spectrum disorders (commentary). *Journal of Autism and Developmental Disorders*, **30**, pp. 391-396.

Lord, C. et al (2000). The Autism Diagnostic Observation Schedule-Generic: a standard measure of social and communication deficits associated with the spectrum of autism. *Journal of Autism and Developmental Disorders*, **30**(3), pp. 205-223.

Lord, C. et al (2001). *Educating children with autism.* Washington D. C: National Research Council.

Lord, C. et al (2002). *Autism Diagnostic Observation Schedule (ADOS) Manual.* Los Angeles, CA: Western Psychological Services.

Lord, C. and Bailey, A. (2002). Autism spectrum disorders. In: M. Rutter and E. Taylor (eds.), *Child and Adolescent Psychiatry*, 4th ed. Oxford: Blackwell Science, pp. 636-663.

Lord, C. and Magill-Evans, J. (1995). Peer interactions of autistic children and adolescents. *Development and Psychopathology*, **7**, pp. 611-626.

Lord, C., Rutter, M., and Le Couteur, A. (1994). Autism Diagnostic Interview—Revised: a revised version of a diagnostic interview for caregivers of individuals with possible pervasive developmental disorders. *Journal of Autism and Developmental Disorders*, **24**(5), pp. 659-685.

Lotter, V. (1966). Epidemiology of autistic conditions in young children: I. Prevalence. *Social Psychiatry*, **1**, pp. 124-137.

Marcus, L., Howlin, P., and Lord, C. (2000). TEACCH services for preschool children. In: Handleman, J. S. and Harris, S. L. (eds.) *Preschool education programs for children with autism.* Austin TX: Pro-Ed Inc.

Mawhood, L. and Howlin, P. (1999). The outcome of a supported employment scheme for high functioning adults with autism or Asperger's Syndrome, *Autism*, **3**, pp. 229-254.

McCarthy, D. (1972) *McCarthy scales of children's abilities.* London: Psychological Corporation.

McConachie, H. et al (1999). How do child development teams work?; Findings from a UK National Survey. *Child: Care, Health and Development*, **25**, pp.101-113.

McDougle C. J. et al (1996). A double-blind, placebo-controlled study of fluoxamine in adults with autistic disorders. *Archives of General Psychiatry*, **53**, pp. 1001-1008.

McDougle, C. J. et al (1998). A double-blind, placebo-controlled study of risperidone in adults with autistic disorder and other pervasive developmental disorders. *Archives of General Psychiatry*, **55**, pp. 633-641.

McDougle, C. J. et al (2000). Background and rationale for an initial controlled study of risperidone. *Child and Adolescent Psychiatric Clinics of North America*, **9**, pp. 201-224.

McEachin, J. J., Smith, T. and Lovaas, O. I. (1993). Long-term outcome for children with autism who received early intensive behavioural treatment. *American Journal on Mental Retardation*, **97**, pp. 359-372.

Medical Research Council (2001). *Review of autism research: epidemiology and causes*. London: MRC.

Mesibov, G. (1997). Formal and informal measures of the effectiveness of the TEACCH Programme. *Autism*, **1**, pp. 25-35.

Mesibov, G., Schopler, E., and Caison, W. (1989). The Adolescent and adult psychoeducational profile: assessment of adolescents and adults with severe developmental handicaps. *Journal of Autism and Developmental Disorders*, **19**, pp. 33-40.

Mudford, O. C., et al. (2000) Auditory integration training for children with autism: no behavioral benefits detected. *American Journal of Mental Retardation*, **105**, pp. 118-129.

Mukherjee, S., Beresford, B., and Sloper, P. (1999). *Unlocking key working: an analysis and evaluation of key worker services for families of disabled children*. Bristol: The Policy Press.

Mullen, E. (1997). *The Mullen Scales of Early Learning* (1997). Circle Pines, Minnesota: American Guidance Service.

Murch, S. (2002) *Paper on children with bowel disorders and autism* presented at the meeting of the All Party Parliamentary Group on Autism, 25th June 2002, London.

Murphy, M. et al (2000). Personality traits of the relatives of autistic probands. *Psychological Medicine*, **30**, pp. 1411-1424.

New York State Department of Health (2000). *Review:* Clinical Practice Guidelines Report of the recommendations – Autism / Pervasive Developmental Disorders, Assessment and Intervention for Young Children (age 0 – 3 years) www.health.state.ny.us/nysdoh/epi/autism

Pfeiffer, S. T. et al (1995). Efficacy of vitamin B6 and magnesium in the treatment of autism: a methodological review and summary of outcomes. *Journal of Autism and Developmental Disorders,* **25**, pp. 481-492.

Piven, J. and Palmer, P. (1999). Psychiatric disorder and the broad autism phenotype: evidence from a family study of multiple-incidence autism families. *American Journal of Psychiatry*, **156**, pp. 557-563.

Powell, A. (2002). *Taking responsibility – good practice guidelines for services for adults with Asperger's Syndrome.* London: National Autistic Society.

Powers, M. (1992). Early intervention for children with autism. In: Berkell, D. (ed.) *Autism: identification, education, and treatment.* Hillsdale, NJ: L. Erlbaum Associates.

Psychopharmacology Bulletin, **26**, pp. 260-266.

Raven, J. (1956). *Guide to using the coloured progressive matrixes*. London: H. K. Lewis.

Reichelt, K. L. et al (1991). Probable etiology and possible treatment of childhood autism. *Brain Dysfunction*, **4**, pp. 308-319.

Rescorla, L., and Schwartz, E. (1990). Outcomes of toddlers with specific expressive language delay. *Applied Psycholinguistics*, **11**, pp. 393-407.

Rogers, S. J. (1996). Early intervention in autism. *Journal of Autism and Developmental Disorders*, **26**, pp. 243-246.

Rogers, S. J. (1998). Empirically supported comprehensive treatments for young children with autism. *Journal of Clinical Child Psychology*, **27**, pp. 168-179.

Rogers, S. J. (2000). Interventions that facilitate socialisation in children with autism. *Journal of Autism and Developmental Disorders*, **30**, pp. 399-410.

Roid, G. and Miller, L. (1997) Leiter-R: *Leiter International Performance Scale revised*. Wood Dale, Illinois: Stoelting Co.

Runco, M. A. and Schreibman, L. (1987). Socially validating behavioural objectives in the treatment of autistic children. *Journal of Autism and Developmental Disorders*, **17**, pp. 141-147.

Rutter, M. (2001). Autism: two-way interplay between research and clinical work. In: *Research and innovation on the road to modern child psychiatry, volume 1: festschrift for Professor Sir Michael Rutter* / edited by Jonathan Green and William Yule. London: Gaskell and the Association of Child Psychology and Psychiatry, pp. 54-80.

Rutter, M. and Bartak, L. (1973). Special educational treatment of autistic children: a comprehensive study 1: design of study and characteristics of units. *Journal of Child Psychology and Psychiatry*, **14**, pp. 161-179.

Rutter, M. and Taylor, E. (2002). *Child and Adolescent Psychiatry*. 4th ed. Blackwell Publishing: Oxford.

Rutter, M., et al (1994). Autism and known medical conditions: myth and substance. *Journal of Child Psychology and Psychiatry and Allied Disciplines*, **35**, pp. 311-322.

Rutter, M., et al (2002). *Social Communication Questionnaire (SCQ)*. Los Angeles, CA: Western Psychological Services.

Sandler A. D. et al (1999). A double blind placebo controlled trial of synthetic human secretin in the treatment of autism and pervasive developmental disorders. *Journal of Developmental and Behavioural Paediatrics,* **20**, p. 400.

Santosh, P. (2000). Neuroimaging in child and adolescent psychiatric disorders. *Archives of Disease in Childhood*, **82**, pp. 412-419.

Santosh, P. and Baird, G. (1999). Psychopharmacotherapy in children and adults with intellectual disability. *Lancet*, **354**, pp. 233-242.

Scambler, D., Rogers, S. J., and Wehner, E. A. (2001). Can the Checklist for autism in toddlers differentiate young children with autism from those with developmental delays? *Journal of the American Academy of Child and Adolescent Psychiatry*, **40**, pp.1457-1463.

Schopler, E. (1997). Implementation of TEACCH Philosophy. In: D. J. Cohen and F. R. Volkmar (eds) *Handbook of Autism and Pervasive Developmental Disorders* 2nd ed, pp 767-798. New York: John Wiley.

Schopler, E. et al. (1990). *Individualized assessment and treatment for autistic and developmentally disabled children,* Vol. 1. Austin TX.: Pro-Ed Inc.

Schopler, E. and Reichler, R.J., (1971). Parents as cotherapists in the treatment of psychotic children. *Journal of Autism and Childhood Schizophrenia*, **1**(1), pp. 87-102.

Schreibman, L. (2000). Intensive behavioural psychoeducational treatments for autism: research needs and future directions. *Journal of Autism and Developmental Disorders,* **30**, pp. 373-378.

Scott, F. et al (2002). Childhood Asperger's Syndrome Test (CAST). *Autism*, **6**, pp. 9-31.

Scott, F., Baron-Cohen, S., and Bolton, P. (2002). Brief report: Prevalence of autism spectrum conditions in children age 5 to 11 years in Cambridgeshire, UK. *Autism*, **6** (3), pp. 231-237.

Shattock, P. (2000). Presentation to NIASA Working Group.

Shevell, M. et al (2001). Etiologic yield of autistic spectrum disorders: a prospective study. *Journal of Child Neurology*, **16**(7), pp. 509-512.

Shields, J. (2001). The NAS EarlyBird Programme: partnership with parents in early intervention. *Autism*, **5**, pp. 49-56.

Siegel, B. (1998). Early screening and diagnosis in autism spectrum disorders: The Pervasive Developmental Disorders Screening Test (PDDST). Paper presented at the *NIH State of Science in Autism Screening and Diagnosis Working Conference*, Bethesda, MD, June 15-17.

Simonoff, E. (2000). Presentation to NIASA Working Group.

Skjeldal, O. H. et al (1998). Childhood autism: the need for physical investigations. *Brain and Development*, **20**, pp. 227-233.

Smalley, S. et al (1995). Autism, affective disorders and social phobia. *American Journal of Medical Genetics*, **60**, pp. 19-26.

Smith, T. (1996). Are other treatments effective? In *Behavioural interventions for young children with autism*, ed, C. Maurice, G. Green and S. C. Luce, pp. 45-59. Austin TX: Pro-Ed inc.

Smith, T. (1999). Outcome of early intervention for children with autism. *Clinical Psychology: Science and Practice*, **6**, pp. 33-49.

Smith, T., Groen, A. D. and Wynn, J. W. (2000). Randomised trial of early intensive intervention for children with pervasive developmental disorder. *American Journal on Mental Retardation*, **105**, pp. 269-285.

Sowter, M., et al (2002). Early communication is "More than words". *Communication*, **36** (1), pp. 35-37.

Sparrow, S. S., Balla, D. A., and Cicchetti, D. V. (1984). *Vineland Adaptive Behavior Scales Interview Edition, Survey Form Manual*. Circle Pines, Minnesota: American Guidance Service (AGS).

Stone, W. L., et al. (1994). Early recognition of autism: parental reports vs clinical observation. *Archives of Pediatrics and Adolescent Medicine*, **148**(2), pp.174-179.

Stone, W. L., et al. (1999). Patterns of adaptive behavior in very young children with autism. *American Journal on Mental Retardation*, **104**(2), pp.187-199.

Strain, P. S., and Hoyson, M. (2000). The need for longitudinal, intensive social skill intervention: LEAP follow-up outcomes for children with autism. *Topics in Early Childhood Special Education*, **20**, pp.116-122.

Stutsman, R. (1948a) *Guide for administering the Merrill Palmer scale of mental tests*. New York: Harcourt, Brace and World.

Stutsman, R. (1948b). *Merrill-Palmer scale of mental tests*. Los Angeles: Western Psychological Services.

Sussman, F. (1999). *More than words: helping parents promote communication and social skills in children with autism spectrum disorders:* Toronto: Hanen Centre.

Szatmari, P. et al (1998). Genetics of autism: overview and new directions. *Journal of Autism and Developmental Disorders*, **28**, pp. 351-368.

Thorndyke, R. L., Hagen, E. and Sattler, J. (1989). *Stanford-Binet intelligence scale*, 4th ed. Windsor: NFER-Nelson.

Tuchman, R. F. and Rapin, I. (1997). Regression in pervasive developmental disorders: seizures and epileptiform electroencephalogram correlates. *Paediatrics*, **99**, pp.560-566.

Tuchman, R. F., Rapin, I. and Shinnar, S. (1991). Autistic and dysphasic children. II: Epilepsy *Pediatrics,* **88**(6), pp.1219-25

Volkmar, F. (1998). Autism and pervasive developmental disorders. *Cambridge Monographs in Child and Adolescent Psychiatry*. Cambridge: Cambridge University Press.

Volkmar, F. R. et al (1999). Practice parameters for the assessment and treatments of children, adolescents and adults with autism and other pervasive developmental disorders. *Journal of the American Academy of Child and Adolescent Psychiatry*, **38**, pp. 325-525.

Watling, R.,L., Deitz, J., White, O. (2000). Comparison of Sensory Profile scores of young children with and without autistic spectrum disorders. *American Journal of Occupational Therapy*, **55**, pp. 416-423.

Wechsler, D. (1990). *Manual for Wechsler pre-school and primary scale of intelligence (Revised British Amendments)*. Sidcup: The Psychological Corporation.

Wechsler, D. (1992). *Manual for the Wechsler intelligence scale for children – (WISC-III UK)*. 3rd ed. Sidcup: Psychological Corporation.

Weiss, M. J. (2002). Hardiness and social support as predictors of stress in mothers of typical children, children with autism and children with mental retardation. *Autism*, **6**(1), pp. 115-130.

Whiteley, P. et al (1999). A gluten free diet as an intervention for autism and associated spectrum disorders: preliminary findings. *Autism*, **3**, pp. 45–66.

Wilson, J., and Jungner, G. (1968). *Principles and practice of screening for disease* Vol. 37. Geneva: WHO.

Wing, L. (1996). Autistic spectrum disorders: no evidence for or against an increase in prevalence. *British Medical Journal*, **312**, pp. 327-328.

Wing, L. (1996). *The autistic spectrum: a guide for parents and professionals*. London: Constable.

Wing, L., et al (2002). The Diagnostic Interview for Social and Communication Disorders: background, reliability and clinical use. *Journal of Child Psychology and Psychiatry and Allied Disciplines*, **43** (3), pp. 307-325.

Wing, L. and Gould, J. (1979). Severe impairments of social interaction and associated abnormalities in children: epidemiology and classification. *Journal of Autism and Developmental Disorders*, **9**, pp.11-29.

Wolfberg, P. J. and Schuler, A. L. (1993). Integrated playgroups: a model for promoting the social and cognitive dimensions of play. *Journal of Autism and Developmental Disorders*, **23**, pp. 1-23.

Woodhouse, W. et al (1996). Head circumference and pervasive developmental disorders. *Journal of Child Psychology and Psychiatry and Allied Disciplines*, **37**, pp. 665-671.

World Health Organisation. (1993). *The International Classification of Diseases: classification of mental and behavioural disorders. Diagnostic criteria for research.* (ICD-10). 10th ed. Geneva: WHO.

Appendix C

Glossary of Terms (in alphabetical order)

ADHD	Attention Deficit Hyperactivity Disorder
ADL	Adaptive living skills
ADI-R	Autistic Diagnostic Interview - Revised
ADOS	Autistic Diagnostic Observational Schedule
AED	Anti epileptic drugs
APA	American Psychiatric Association
APPGA	All Party Parliamentary Group Chair: Dr Stephen Ladyman, MP
ASD	Autistic Spectrum Disorder
BACCH	British Association of Community Child Health
BCS	Base Clinical Services
BPS	British Psychological Society
CAMHS	Child and Adolescent Mental Health Service
Care manager	(See 4.3.2.1) A care manager is envisaged as being actively involved in the assessment for provision of services and advocacy for the family (Disability EWG for National Service Framework for children)
CARS	Childhood Autism Rating Scale
CAST	Childhood Asperger's Syndrome Test
CCST	Consultant Certificate for Specialist Training
CDS	Child Development Service(s)
CHAT	CHecklist for Autism in Toddlers
CHS	Child Health Surveillance
CTLD/CLDT	Community Team for Learning Disabilities
CLDS	Community Learning Disability Services
COSPPA	The Confederation of Service Providers for People with Autism
CPD	Continuing Professional Development
CPK	Creatinine Phosphokinase
CT	Computerised Tomography
DISCO	Diagnostic Interview for Social and Communication Disorders
DfES	Department for Education and Skills
DoH	Department of Health
DNA	Deoxyribonucleic Acid
DSM-IV	Diagnostic and Statistical Manual IV 4th Edition (American Psychiatric Association)
EEG	Electroencephalogram
ESES	Electrical Status Epilepticus during Slow Wave Sleep

FCP	Family Care Plan
Fragile X	Fragile X Chromosomal Anomaly
GDA	General developmental assessment
HEI	Higher Education Institute
IAG	Indolylacryloylglycine
IBD	Intestinal Bowel Disorder/Inflammatory Bowel Disease
ICD-10	The ICD-10 Classification of Mental and Behavioural Disorders (See end of glossary) for F84 Pervasive Developments Disorders
IEP	Individual Education Plan
IQ	Intelligence Quotient

Key worker (See 4.3.1)

Person who:
- has specialist knowledge of autistic spectrum disorders
- has dedicated time
- relates to the child and family
- offers liaison
- is able to take an overview
- has the ability to recognise need
- is able to work collaboratively
- is skilled in team working
- recognises that the child is the focus
- is an advocate for the child.

The key worker will be part of the team that is involved with the child and family to:
- ensure follow up support, especially in relation to post-diagnosis issues and behaviour management
- ensure guidelines are in place to enable all people involved with the child to work consistently
- recognise when short breaks are necessary and, if necessary, negotiate this
- help parents prepare for children's long term needs
- co-ordinate the transition from children's services to adult services
- co-ordinate service provision and ensure that management plans are followed. (This should include all the child's needs and interventions.)

By permission of the Warwickshire Social Development Team (English, 2002)

LAS	Local Autistic Society
LEA	Local Education Authority
LPU	Local Population Unit (or Local Area)
	Refers to the geographical area usually referred to for Health Services provision. The area may or may not be coterminous with Social Services or Education areas. Such Units typically comprise a local population of approximately 55,000 children under sixteen with 4000 births per year. This definition of a local population unit/local area is comparable to the previous health terminology of 'district' It is helpful for service

delivery for Health, Education and Social Services to have coterminous boundaries. However, it is often the case that Health Trusts and Primary Care Trusts may work across geographical areas served by more than one local authority.

MAA	Multi-Agency Assessment
MD	Multi-Disciplinary
MMR	Measles, Mumps and Rubella Immunisation
MRC	Medical Research Council
MRI	Magnetic Resonance Imaging
NAS	National Autistic Society
NSF	National Service Framework
OCD	Obsessive Compulsive Disorder
PBS	Positive Behaviour Support Systems
PCT	Primary Care Trust
PDD	Pervasive Developmental Disorders
PDDST	Pervasive Developmental Disorders Screening Test
PECS	Picture Exchange Communication System
PEDS	Parent Evaluation of Developmental Status
PEP-R	Psychoeducational Profile Revised
PKU	Phenylketonuria
RCPCH	Royal College of Paediatrics and Child Health
RCPsych	Royal College of Psychiatrists
SCQ	Social Communication Questionnaire
SEN	Special Educational Needs
SENCO	Special Educational Needs Co-ordinator
SLT	Speech and Language Therapists
SSRI	Selective Serotonin Reuptake Inhibitors
TEACCH	Treatment and Education of Autistic and Communication Handicapped Children
TS	Tuberous Sclerosis
TTA	Teachers Training Agency
WHO	World Health Organisation
WTE	whole time equivalent

ICD-10 DEFINITION (1993)

F 84 Pervasive developmental disorders

This group of disorders is characterised by qualitative abnormalities in reciprocal social interactions and in patterns of communication, and by restricted, stereotyped, repetitive repertoire of interests and activities. These qualitative abnormalities are a pervasive feature of the individual's functioning in all situations, although they may vary in degree. In most cases, development is abnormal from infancy and, with only a few exceptions, the conditions become manifest during the first 5 years of life. It is usual, but not invariable, for there to be some degree of general cognitive impairment but the disorders are defined in terms of behaviour that is deviant in relation to mental age (whether the individual is retarded or not). There is some disagreement on the subdivision of this overall group of pervasive development disorders.

In some cases the disorders are associated with, and presumably due to, some medical condition, of which infantile spasms, congenital rubella, tuberous sclerosis, cerebral lipidosis, and the fragile X chromosome anomaly are among the most common. However, the disorder should be diagnosed on the basis of the behavioural features, irrespective of the presence or absence of any associated medical conditions; any such associated condition must, nevertheless be separately coded. If mental retardation is present, it is important that it too should be separately coded, under F70 - F79, because it is not a universal feature of the pervasive developmental disorders.

F84.0 Childhood autism

A pervasive developmental disorder defined by the presence of abnormal and/or impaired development that is manifest before the age of 3 years, and by the characteristic type of abnormal functioning in all three areas of social interaction, communication, and restricted, repetitive behaviour. The disorder occurs in boys three to four times more often than in girls.

Diagnostic guidelines

Usually there is no prior period of unequivocally normal development but, if there is, abnormalities become apparent before the age of 3 years. There are always qualitative impairments in reciprocal social interaction. These take the form of an inadequate appreciation of socio-emotional cues, as shown by a lack of responses to other people's emotions and/or a lack of modulation of behaviour according to social context; poor use of social signals and a weak integration of social, emotional, and communicative behaviours; and, especially, a lack of socio-emotional reciprocity. Similarly, qualitative impairments in communications are universal. These take the form of a lack of social usage of whatever language skills are present; impairment in make-believe and social imitative play; poor synchrony and lack of reciprocity in conversational interchange; poor flexibility in language expression and a relative lack of creativity and fantasy in thought processes; lack of emotional response to other people's verbal and nonverbal overtures; impaired use of variations in cadence or emphasis to reflect communicative modulation; and a similar lack of accompanying gesture to provide emphasis or aid meaning in spoken communication.

The condition is also characterised by restricted, repetitive, and stereotyped patterns of behaviour, interests, and activities. These take the form of a tendency to impose rigidity and routine on a wide range of aspects of day-to day functioning; this usually applies to novel activities as well as to familiar habits and play patterns. In early childhood particularly, there may be specific attachment to unusual, typically non-soft objects. The children may insist on the performance of particular routines in rituals of a non-functional character; there may be stereotyped preoccupations with interests such as dates, routes or timetables; often there are motor stereotypes; a specific interest in non functional elements of objects (such as their smell or feel) is common; and there may be a resistance to changes in routine or in details of the personal environment (such as the movement of ornaments or furniture in the family home).

In addition to these specific diagnostic features, it is frequent for children with autism to show a range of other non specific problems such as fear/phobias, sleeping and eating disturbances, temper tantrums, and aggression. Self-injury (e.g. by wrist-biting) is fairly common, especially when there is associated severe mental retardation. Most individuals with autism lack spontaneity, initiative, and creativity in the organization of their leisure time and have difficulty applying conceptualisations in decision-making in work (even when the tasks themselves are well within their capacity). The specific manifestation of deficits characteristic of autism change as the children grow older, but the deficits continue into and through adult life with a broadly similar pattern of problems in socialization, communication, and interest patterns. Developmental abnormalities must have been present in the first 3 years for the diagnosis to be made, but the syndrome can be diagnosed in all age groups.

All levels of IQ can occur in association with autism, but there is significant mental retardation in some three-quarters of cases.

Includes: autistic disorder infantile autism
               infantile psychosis
               Kanner's syndrome

Differential diagnosis. Apart from the other varieties of pervasive developmental disorder it is important to consider: specific developmental disorder of receptive language (F80.2) with secondary socio-emotional problems; reactive attachment disorder (F94. 1) or disinhibited attachment disorder (F94.2); mental retardation (F70-F79) with some associated emotional/behavioural disorder; schizophrenia (F20.) of unusually early onset; and Rett's syndrome (F84.2).

F84.1 Atypical autism

A pervasive developmental disorder that differs from autism in terms either of age of onset or of failure to fulfil all three sets of diagnostic criteria. Thus, abnormal and/or impaired development becomes manifest for the first time only after age 3 years; and/or there are insufficient demonstrable abnormalities in one or two of the three areas of psychopathology required for the diagnosis of autism (namely, reciprocal social interactions, communication, and restrictive, stereotyped, repetitive behaviour) in spite of characteristic abnormalities in the other area(s). Atypical autism arises most often in profoundly retarded individuals whose very low level of functioning provides little scope for exhibition of the specific deviant behaviours required for the diagnosis of autism; it also occurs in individuals with a severe specific developmental disorder of receptive language. Atypical autism thus constitutes a meaningfully separate condition from autism.

Includes: atypical childhood psychosis
               mental retardation with autistic features

F84.2 Rett's syndrome

A condition of unknown cause, so far reported only in girls, which has been differentiated on the basis of a characteristic onset, course, and pattern of symptomatology. Typically, apparently normal or near-normal early development is followed by partial or complete loss of acquired hand skills and of speech, together with deceleration in head growth, usually with an onset between 7 and 24 months of age. Hand-wringing stereotypes, hyperventilation and loss of purposive hand movements are particularly characteristic. Social and play development are arrested in the first 2 or 3 years, but social interest tends to be maintained. During middle childhood, trunk ataxia and apraxia, associated with scoliosis or kyphoscoliosis tend to develop and sometimes there are choreoathetoid movements. Severe mental handicap invariably results. Fits frequently develop during early or middle childhood.

Diagnostic guidelines

In most cases onset is between 7 and 24 months of age. The most characteristic feature is a loss of purposive hand movements and acquired fine motor manipulative skills. This is accompanied by loss, partial loss or lack of development of language; distinctive stereotyped tortuous wringing or 'hand-washing' movements, with the arms flexed in front of the chest or chin; stereotypic wetting of the hands with saliva; lack of proper chewing of food; often episodes of hyperventilation; almost always a failure to gain bowel and bladder control; often excessive drooling and protrusion of the tongue; and a loss of social engagement. Typically, the children retain a kind of 'social smile', looking at or 'through' people but not interact socially with them in early childhood (although social interaction often develops later). The stance and gait tend to become broad-based, the muscles are hypotonic, trunk movements usually become poorly coordinated, and scoliosis or kyphoscoliosis usually develops. Spinal atrophies, with severe motor disability, develop in adolescence or adulthood in about half the cases. Later, rigid spasticity may become manifest, and is usually more pronounced in the lower than in the upper limbs. Epileptic fits, usually involving some type of minor attack, and with an onset generally before the age of 8 years, occur in the majority of cases. In contrast to autism, both deliberate self-injury and complex stereotyped preoccupations or routines are rare.

Differential diagnosis. Initially, Rett's syndrome is differentiated primarily on the basis of the lack of purposive hand movements, deceleration of head growth, ataxia stereotypic 'hand-washing' movements, and lack of proper chewing. The course of the disorder, in terms of progressive motor deterioration, confirms the diagnosis.

F84.3 Other childhood disintegrative disorder

A pervasive developmental disorder (other than Rett's syndrome) that is defined by a period of normal development before onset, and by a definite loss, over the course of a few months, of previously acquired skills in at least several areas of development, together with the onset of characteristic abnormalities of social, communicative, and behavioural functioning. Often there is a prodromic period of vague illness; the child becomes restive, irritable, anxious, and overactive. This is followed by impoverishment and then loss of speech and language, accompanied by behavioural disintegration. In some cases the loss of skills is persistently progressive (usually when the disorder is associated with a progressive diagnosable neurological condition), but more often the decline over a period of some months is followed by a plateau and then a limited improvement. The prognosis is usually very poor, and most individuals are left with severe mental retardation. There is uncertainty about the extent to which this condition differs from autism. In some cases the disorder can be shown to be due to some associated encephalopathy but the diagnosis should be made on the behavioural features. Any associated neurological condition should be separately coded.

Diagnostic guidelines

Diagnosis is based on an apparently normal development up to the age of at least 2 years followed by a definite loss of previously acquired skills this is accompanied by qualitatively abnormal social functioning. It is usual for there to be a profound regression in, or loss of, language, a regression in the level of play, social skills, and adaptive behaviour, and often a loss of bowel or bladder control, sometimes with a deteriorating motor control. Typically, this is accompanied by a general loss of interest in the environment, by stereotyped, repetitive motor mannerism and by an autistic-like impairment of social interaction and communication. In some respects, the syndrome resembles dementia in adult life, but it differs in three key respects there is usually no evidence of any identifiable organic disease or damage (although organic brain dysfunction of some type is usually inferred); the loss of skills may be followed by a degree of recovery and the impairment in socialization and communication has deviant qualities typical of autism rather than of intellectual decline. For all these reasons the syndrome is included here rather than under FOO-F09.

Includes: dementia infantilis
disintegrative psychosis
Heller's syndrome
symbiotic psychosis

Excludes: acquired aphasia with epilepsy (F80.3)
elective mutism (F94.O)
Rett's syndrome (F84.2)
schizophrenia (F20.-)

F84.4 Overactive disorder associated with mental retardation and stereotyped movements

This is an ill-defined disorder of uncertain nosological validity. The category is included here because of the evidence that children with moderate to severe mental retardation (IQ below 50) who exhibit major problems in hyperactivity and inattention frequently show stereotyped behaviours; such children tend not to benefit from stimulant drugs (unlike those with an IQ in the normal range) and may exhibit a severe dysphoric reaction (sometimes with psychomotor retardation) when given stimulants; in adolescence the over activity tends to be replaced by under activity (a pattern that is not usual in hyperkinetic children with normal intelligence). It is also common for the syndrome to be associated with a variety of developmental delays, either specific or global.

The extent to which the behavioural pattern is a function of low IQ or of organic brain damage is not known, neither is it clear whether the disorders in children with mild mental retardation who show the hyperkinetic syndrome would be better classified here or under F90. -; at present they are included in F90.

Diagnostic guidelines

Diagnosis depends on the combination of developmentally inappropriate severe over activity, motor stereotypes, and moderate to severe mental retardation; all three must be present for the diagnosis. If the diagnostic criteria for F84.0, F84.1 or F84.2 are met, that condition should be diagnosed instead.

F84.5 Asperger's syndrome

A disorder of uncertain nosological validity, characterized by the same kind of qualitative abnormalities of reciprocal social interaction that typify autism, together with a restricted, stereotyped, repetitive repertoire of interests and activities. The disorder differs from autism primarily in that there is no general delay or retardation in language or in cognitive development. Most individuals are of normal general intelligence but it is common for them to be markedly clumsy; the condition occurs predominantly in boys (in a ratio of about eight boys to one girl). It seems highly likely that at least some cases represent mild varieties of autism, but it is uncertain whether or not that is so for all. There is a strong tendency for the abnormalities to persist into adolescence and adult life and it seems that they represent individual characteristics that are not greatly affected by environmental influences. Psychotic episodes occasionally occur in early adult life.

Diagnostic guidelines

Diagnosis is based on the combination of a lack of any clinically significant general delay in language or cognitive development plus, as with autism, the presence of qualitative deficiencies in